THE MANUAL OF THE

MARTIAL ARTS

RON VAN CLIEF

RAWSON, WADE PUBLISHERS, INC.
NEW YORK

Library of Congress Cataloging in Publication Data

Van Clief, Ron.
   The manual of martial arts.

   Includes index.
   1. Martial arts.   I. Title.
GV1101.V36   796.8   81-8645
ISBN 0-89256-205-6 (pbk.)   AACR2

Copyright © 1981 by Ron Van Clief
All rights reserved
Published simultaneously in Canada by McClelland and Stewart, Ltd.
Manufactured in the United States of America

Photographs by Bert Torchia and Bill Peck
Cover by Bert Torchia

Credits for movie stills and nostalgia photos:

Aquarius Films
Madison World Films
Silverstein Films

Assistants credits:

Dean Brockway, Melanie Beck, Ron Van Clief Jr., Jeffrey Craig
S. Filson, Danny Gwira, Ivory Lewis, Maurice J. Miller,
Glen Perry, Wilson Ramirez, Millie Tirado, Danny Witherspoon

Designed by Jacques Chazaud

Second Printing July 1982

Contents

1	Introduction to the Martial Arts	9
2	The Psycho-Physical Conditioning Process: "The Warm Up"	17
3	Hand Techniques	25
4	The Black Dragon Blocking System	55
5	Leg Techniques	71
6	Strategy and Tactics	101
7	Self-Defense for Women	113
8	Self-Defense for Senior Citizens	143
9	Martial Arts Education for Children	153
10	Advanced Self-Defense	161
11	The Alphabet of Martial Arts	171
Appendix:	The World Masters in Action Awards	181
Index		185

THE MANUAL OF THE MARTIAL ARTS

1. Introduction to the Martial Arts (Origin, Objectives, and Principles)

What are the martial arts? "Martial arts" is a collective term, meaning the art of self-defense. In the following chapters, I will introduce you to the basic concepts and principles of the four major forms of martial arts—karate, kung fu, Tae Kwon Do, and aiki jitsu. Martial arts have been around since the beginning of time; the dinosaurs became extinct, but man survived because of his uncanny ability to adapt to the environment. Survival is the first instinct of human beings. The dinosaur died because of its inability to reason. Reason is the process of systematic logic and deductive analysis, and logic is the byproduct of perceptual experience. Thus we have understanding. Life is in fact a series of understandings and experiences. The environment dictates to the organism what the behavioral pattern will be. A proper martial arts training should teach the student to increase his or her human growth potential during the life cycle. The martial arts are 90 percent mental and 10 percent physical.

The word *karate* is Japanese for empty hand, and karate itself is a martial art of unarmed self-defense in which blows of the hand or feet are directed from poised positions. A special technique of breathing is used, and shouts known as the "kiai" accompany the blows. But karate is more than simply a method of combat. It is a highly developed system of self-discipline, positive attitudes, and intense moral purpose.

The roots of the martial arts are in Asia: it was first used as a monastic training, and later became a means by which Chinese peasants could defend themselves against armed bandits. Karate as we know it today developed during the seventeenth century on the island of Okinawa, the largest of the Ryuku chain that stretches south from Japan to the East China Sea. For many centuries Okinawa was ruled by a succession of regimes that banned the use of all weapons among the populace. An effort to ensure control over the people, this prohibition on weapons contributed in a major way to the rapid development of the "empty hand" method of self-defense. A rural people whose lives were paced by changing seasons and the harvest of their crops, the Okinawans wished

to live peacefully, but without any weapons they felt insecure and vulnerable. Their hands were the most readily available means by which to protect themselves, and thus they developed the "weaponless weapon." Kung fu is said to have originated early in the sixth century when a Buddhist monk, Daruma, crossed the treacherous Himalaya Mountains—a landscape alive with outlaws, cutthroats, and wild animals, and plagued by inclement weather. Daruma developed the technique to propagate his religious teachings in China. He observed the movements and fighting habits of the great cats, other wild animals, even the tiniest insects, and formed from his observations a method of self-defense as natural as that of the animals themselves.

Fishermen and gamblers in coastal cities became especially well known for their excellent striking and kicking techniques. Persons from the upper classes, also forbidden to use weapons, noted the techniques of self-defense employed by the lower classes and sought to learn them, too. Over the years, these techniques were refined and improved upon, and arranged in logical and systematic patterns, but it was centuries before they were written down. Because the martial arts were illegal, their study was conducted in secret, and information was passed on orally from teacher to student. The close relationship between karate teacher and student was developed in this way.

Throughout Asia many styles and philosophies emerged, but all kept in common one element: the integration of the body and mind into a "weaponless weapon." Thus, in China, chuan fa or gung fu—the major Chinese precursor of karate—sprang up. Elsewhere, as in Southeast Asia, other forms of the weaponless weapon arose, for example, pentjak and silat. *Gung fu* and *kung fu* are Mandarin and Cantonese terms respectively, and refer to the same art. I will be using the two terms throughout the manual to familiarize the student with both of them; but keep in mind that they have the same meaning. It is often held that karate or a type of kung fu was introduced to Okinawa from China during the T'ang Dynasty (A.D. 618 to 907). The ancient Okinawan style of combat was called "Kempo." But through the influences of the mainland, Okinawan-style karate as it is known today was introduced somewhere between 1784 and 1903.

In 1915, karate was brought to Japan by Master Gichin Funakoshi. Another Okinawan master, Chojun Miyagi, lectured and taught his art at Kyoto Imperial University, introducing the Japanese to both the hard and soft elements of a style of karate known as Goju. *Ju* means fifty in Japanese, revealing that there were originally fifty diversified hard and soft techniques of hand and foot strikes. By 1930, when Professor Gogen Yamaguchi organized the first Goju federation, Goju had become thoroughly Japanese. In 1955, Master Peter Urban, after long study in Japan with Masters Yamaguchi, Mas Oyama, and Dr. Richard Kim, brought the Goju style to the United States and organized the first American federation of Goju stylists, under the title U.S.A. Goju. Masters Frank Ruiz and Harry Rosenstein, disciples of Master Urban, broke off from the parent organization in 1965 in order to start the Nisei Goju System. (The Japanese word *Nisei* means second generation.)

The metamorphosis of the Goju style is still continuing. In 1973, this author founded and organized Chinese Goju in America. Chinese Goju is a further development in the martial arts in the United States since it incorporates the diversity of many related martial arts around the central core of the Goju style. Chinese Goju is a total martial arts concept, combining the Eastern and Western philosophies. The technique develops the personality of the student through proper mental and physical conditioning. Martial arts ideology evolves with the environment and is directly related to man's phenomenal ability to adapt. Chinese Goju combines Chinese and Japanese ideology with American ingenuity, teaching fluidity and flexibility of both mind and body for full human development.

Karate training is an experience that builds the body, strengthens the mind, and enriches the spirit. The ultimate aim is to bring mind and spirit together with the body in perfect unison—the Japanese word for this ideal oneness is *zen*. The development of physical power through karate is less important than the development of mental power and self-discipline. The emphasis on the mind as well as the body serves to increase the karate student's sense of awareness and an ability to cope with the environment. One of the greatest assets derived from karate training is the ability to know oneself.

There are also other rewards. The karate practitioner who learns to function under stress finds that he or she is better able to function well in normal circumstances too. The positive conditioning that results from proper karate training allows the student to remain calm and relaxed in any situation. Studies have shown that pain is greater when a person is tense and that it decreases when a person relaxes. Accordingly, the person trained to relax has an added measure of confidence that is invaluable in day-to-day living.

Proper coordination of mind and body is the ultimate goal of the martial artist. Once the beginner has mastered the basic physical mechanics of technique, he or she is in a position to apply those techniques through coordinated kicking and striking combinations. The development of fluidity and continuity is necessary to any student who seeks to become proficient in sparring or actual combat. The ability to execute a particular technique is a small part of the art of karate; the person who is physically superior does not always win the contest. A strike or thrust at the wrong time can prove as detrimental as not being able to execute any technique at all. Thus there are three elements integral to power: speed, timing, and focus. Speed is achieved through training and practice. Timing is acquired through sparring and "kata," or the practice of forms. Focus is the ability to hit the target with maximum concentrated energy. Speed, timing, and focus are necessary for power; practice is necessary for speed, timing, and focus.

The most important technique the student of karate must learn is blocking, or the art of not getting hit. It is impossible to execute any technique if the student is knocked out first. Blocking is the ability to thwart, impede, or deflect the opponent's attack and prepare the attacker for a counterattack, or to position him so that he can continue the attack. Basic blocking drills are practiced with both hands simultaneously and in a shoulder-width stance. There are two basic blocking systems—the hard blocking system and the soft blocking system. The hard blocking system involves a high energy output of strength and force. The attacker can be injured by proper execution of the hard block; however, such a block is not always functional. The soft blocking system is particularly suited to women and children because it involves a low energy output. The soft block involves the use of the opponent's forward motion to deflect the attack and put the attacker off balance. The saving of energy in using the soft block allows for a maximum output of energy in the counterattack. It is useful, too, when there are multiple attackers.

When the blocking techniques are executed correctly, counterattacks are easier to perform. The block complements the counter by forcing the attacker to commit himself. Hard blocks are used to stop an attack by force by injuring the assailant's striking limb—the shin, knee, or elbow. And, too, the shock of the block gives a person time to counterattack. "Critical distance" is important in blocking: when blocking, the movement is forward, the object being to keep the opponent within punching or kicking range. The greater the distance between a person and his or her opponent, the more momentum the opponent has. But there are situations when a greater distance is advantageous; for example, if the opponent is advancing, his weight at some instant is on the primary or forward limb. This is the perfect condition for executing a sweep of the attacker. The proper execution of the block and counter involves three components: speed is required to stop the attacker; eye training is necessary to evaluate correctly the opponent's distance and fighting stance; and focus is involved in the ability to hit the target with maximum concentrated energy.

After the student, or karate-ka, has begun to develop a blocking system, he or she is in a position to concentrate on hand techniques, which are invaluable in both sparring and actual combat. The hand is quicker and more accurate than the leg; furthermore, the hand can be used effectively at close range, particularly in confined situations when it is impossible to use leg techniques. There

is virtually no situation in which a hand technique cannot be applied. In drilling the basic hand techniques, the shoulder-width stance is used. Hand techniques are executed in slow motion and at shoulder height. Strikes and punches are focused and executed directly to the front. After the techniques have been practiced in slow motion, they are executed at full speed. Some commonly employed hand techniques are the sunfist, the iron elbow, the iron palm, the tiger claw, and the snake fist.

The legs have less dexterity than the hands, but leg techniques are stronger and cover more distance. The student who wishes to become proficient in karate must develop his leg techniques to the fullest extent. They are ideally used in coordination with circular combinations in sparring and actual combat. In developing proper leg techniques, emphasis should be placed on the cocking position, called the "chamber," in which the knee is raised. This is a preparatory position for most kicking maneuvers. Emphasis also should be placed on the bending of the supporting leg, to ensure balance. In sparring, a person should never be farther from his opponent than a leg's distance. For maximum application, kicks should be extended from the stomach downward. The best application of hand techniques, by comparison, is from the groin area upward.

Basic sparring or actual combat is an integral part of karate training. In order to become proficient, the student must develop three component abilities. The first is referred to as "maintaining critical distance," and it involves the ability to strike or kick the opponent at will. Next, it is necessary to create an opening. To create a face opening, for example, the opponent should be attacked with a groin or low-area kick, followed by hand techniques to the face area. To create an opening in the low area—examples are the groin, knee, or stomach—a face punch should be thrown and followed by a low-level kick. The third component

ability in basic sparring, or actual combat, is the block-and-counter application. In the Chinese Goju, blocking and countering are done in one motion. The Black Dragon Blocking System is the essence of the Chinese Goju System. This drill teaches how to effectively block and counter your opponent's offensive action.

All offensive and defensive techniques must be practiced until they become completely automatic. Thinking is the pause between action and reaction—let your body and mind flow together. Always remember that martial arts are a science, subject to the laws of physics and physiology. Martial arts are the key to inner freedom and positive emotional expression. Always look, listen, and think. The golden rule for the study of self-defense is "Don't get hit!" Avoid getting hit with various blocking devices and evasive action such as sidestepping and body shifting.

All beginners are known as White Belts; Green Belts have at least six months training, Purple Belts one year, Brown Belts one and a half to two years. First Degree Black Belts must train a minimum of three years. A Red Belt requires a minimum of twenty years.

There are six levels in the belt-ranking system in the Chinese Goju style. There are also eight degrees of Black Belt and two degrees of Red Belt. The first and second degrees of Black Belt mean you are a serious student. The third degree is a qualified teacher; below the third degree is considered an instructor (there is a great deal of difference between an instructor and a teacher). The third degree is called "sensei" (pronounced CEN-SAY) and the sensei is the head of the school. The fourth and fifth degrees are "master teachers," whose position is that of renshi. The color of the renshi belt is red and white. The sixth, seventh, and eighth degrees wear red belts with a thin black line down the middle. These levels are normally honorary degrees, reserved for martial arts educators. The ninth and tenth degrees are the foundation of the system. This level is known as kyoshi (pronounced KEY-OH-SHE and means "Professor" in Japanese). It is reserved for the founder or creator of the system.

But rank has no real meaning, being merely an evaluation of your mental and physical abilities. Study not for rank, but for knowledge! The study of martial arts can be a rewarding experience. Be sure to select a practical style and a competent instructor. This manual will give you the ability to determine the validity of a particular style and the quality of the instruction. In the past twenty-five years I have seen and experienced many different forms of martial arts. Every art has a distinct personality. Choose the style that works for you. Good luck in your studies, and may the force be with you!

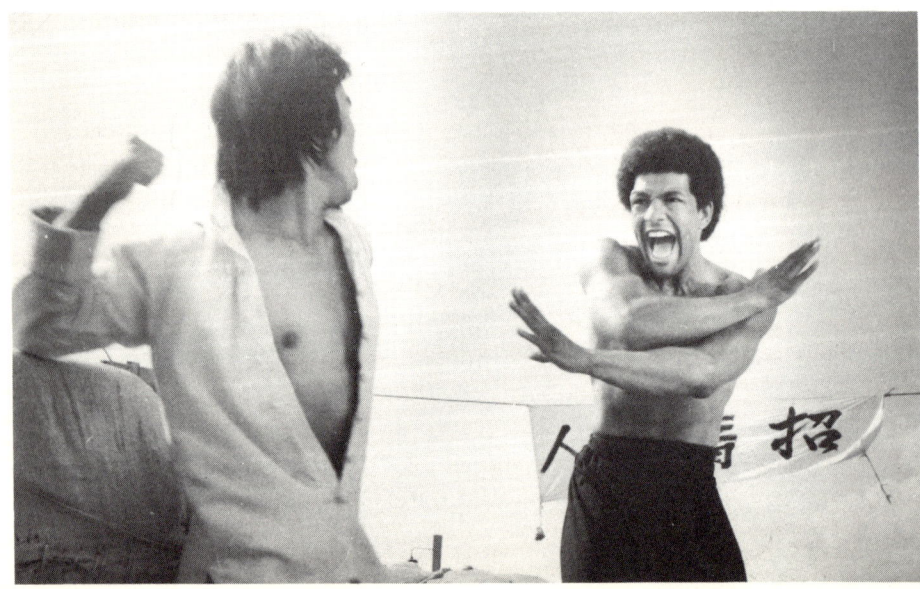

2. The Psycho-Physical Conditioning Process: "The Warm Up"

The study of the martial arts is a total effort of physical and psychological energies concentrated for complete development. Psychology may be defined as the study of the mind and of human and animal behavior. Martial arts psychology is the study of the mind and of human nature. Martial arts education gives us a greater insight and the ability for complete emotional expression. Those of us who study the martial arts have gained not only the ability to defend ourselves but the inner satisfaction that comes from physical and mental harmony acquired through our training. These benefits far exceed our initial evaluation of the martial arts. Karate, kung fu, and judo are all psycho-sciences—sciences dealing with the mind and mental behavior.

The warm-up must be a combination of mental and physical drills that modify the behavior patterns of the student. If learning is psychological inquiry, then we must first understand our reasons for studying the arts of self-defense. We are living in a dangerous society in which the national fear index is so high that as people we exist in a state of virtual paranoia. Fear is not the only motivation, but it ranks very high. Still, it is my opinion that people are becoming more aware of themselves and their relationship to physical fitness. Physical fitness and nutrition are already household words. The government should institute a national physical fitness program that would include martial arts education. Americans are No. 1 in sports and sciences. Why not have an overall program that would start when children are in grade school and continue throughout college and university? Right now in the United States today there are over ten thousand schools of the martial arts; there are karate, Tae Kwon Do, and judo clubs at most colleges and universities. It is up to all martial artists to reflect a serious attitude toward the martial arts. Martial arts should never be played with. Always train under supervision and never exceed your limitations. Remember, we are all human and have limitations.

The training process starts with basic exercises to develop flexibility, speed, and strength. Next in the training schedule comes the psycho-physical conditioning process—the development of our human resources. Stamina, coordination, emotional content, and discipline are all necessary components for the study of the martial arts. Our bodies are living machines that require maintenance, just like our cars, bikes, and skates. We need our bodies to last for a lifetime, so we must take the best care of them possible. Exercise is maintenance for our minds and bodies. Just like a car, we must be tuned up. Martial arts can tune your whole body up. The mental and physical drills develop your overall capacity for life. And everyone must learn how to relax to achieve any benefit from martial skills.

There are numerous drills that teach how to breathe properly. Until quite recently, the most popular methods for expanding muscle development have been based on isometric and isotonic exercising—isometric refers to muscular contraction through resistance without movement, i.e., exerting pressure against an immovable object. This technique is advantageous for the development of a specific muscle area, but is insufficient for developing the entire length of a muscle fiber. In direct contrast to this principle is isotonics—resistance with movement. By contracting a muscle against a moving object, the fibers are shortened and the workload is extended. But isotonics has a limitation, because as the leverage advantage increases, there is a loss of resistance. For instance, when an exerciser lifts a weight, the resistance is lessened as his momentum increases and the lever action of his arm is shortened.

Through the principle of isokinetics, this loss of resistance is eliminated. Simply speaking, isokinetics, as demonstrated through the application of the martial arts, provides exercise wherein the resistance to the contracting muscles is constant and more uniform throughout the full range of motion. If your intent is to build endurance and increase your cardiovascular capacity, reduce the resistance and perform your repetitions rapidly. Physiologically speaking, martial arts are the perfect exercise. The resistance factor builds strength while at the same time the sustained, rhythmical motion increases and maintains cardiovascular and respiratory involvement—another reason why the study of the martial arts is the ultimate in modern exercising.

The ideal exercising session should last ten to fifteen minutes, followed by practice of form and technical application. When you start the process of keeping physically fit, you must realize that it is a continual process of maintaining yourself. It is not hard to get in good shape; it *is* hard to stay there. And remember, the older you get, the harder it is to get in shape and to stay in shape. Once you get in shape, it is best to stay that way for life.

Exercise can be used as a gauge by which to estimate your physical abilities. Never over-exercise; it is wise to do everything in moderation. Before starting martial arts or any program of physical conditioning, it is best to have a physical checkup by your doctor. The next step is to find a competent instructor. Be careful when selecting a place to study. Although there are many names for the places where we study our art, the most common is the dojo. The word "dojo" is Japanese in its origins. Tae Kwon Do or Korean karate students call their place of study the "dojang," kung fu people call their temple a "kwoon." It really is the same place and is sacred to all students of the martial arts.

Finally, there is no perfect form of martial arts. After all, it is people who make a system work, not the system that makes the people work. So, study to develop your own potential, not to imitate or compete with anyone. Let go of all ego and your energy will continually flow. Physical maintenance is a lifetime occupation. Relax and open your mind to be receptive to the art and the environment. It is a mistake to assume that practice makes perfect. First, there is no perfection, and second, it is proper practice that achieves technical ability. The initial conditioning of the martial arts student is aimed at achieving a proper mental attitude. It is helpful for students to think of the human body as a machine: the arms and legs, for example, can be thought of as spokes in their relationship to the wheel. With this in mind, the martial artist begins the tedious job of conditioning his or her body. The combination of exercises that follows will make your body more agile and more powerful.

THE PUSH-UP

Opening Posture—The push-up is a tremendous overall exercise that develops the shoulders, chest, back, and upper arms. Stand with your heels together and hands next to the outside of your body. Before you start your exercise, it is most important to relax your mind so that your body can work without mental tensions. Remember to start slowly and breathe correctly. Always breathe normally; never hold your breath when exercising. Breathe in through your nose and exhale through your mouth.

Starting Position—Your back should be straight to achieve the maximum benefit of the push-up. Hands should be placed directly beneath the shoulders for proper muscle-group usage. Start to lower yourself slowly to the floor. You should be inhaling as you start the downward motion.

Maximum Output Phase—As soon as you touch the floor with your chest, immediately start to exhale as you push your body up to the full extension of both arms. It is essential to coordinate the pushing action with the exhalation. Try to develop a natural flow with the upward and downward motions. It is important to try to do as many repetitions as possible every time you do any exercise. In the early stages of psycho-physical training, the number of repetitions should be from 8 to 10 for each set. You should not rest more than 1 minute between sets of exercises. Stamina and endurance are more mental than physical. Psycho-phyiscal training conditions the mind and body to work together for maximum efficiency.

THE JACK KNIFE

Starting Position—The jackknife is the most important of all the exercises for total physical fitness. The main areas of development are the mind and the abdominal muscles. The abdomen or "midsection" is the most crucial part of the body. Located here are many vital organs that control the body's health and well-being. The stomach, liver, kidneys, bladder, bowels, intestines, etc., all carry on their owner's best interest in this region. A few minutes a day spent in abdominal exercise will pay you splendid dividends. There are over 50 different exercises for the abdomen, but the jackknife is one of my favorites. This exercise starts in the supine position with the legs as close together as possible. Place both hands palm upward on the floor above your head. The objective is to bring the hands and feet as close together as possible. It is very important to start your hands and feet upward at the same time.

Maximum Output Phase—As you start up, remember to keep your feet as close together as possible. Inhale as you start up, exhale as you start down. Try your best to touch your fingers to your toes. This exercise takes a lot of mental determination and physical stamina, but is definitely worth the extra effort.

Important Points to Remember—Always start out slowly when doing any exercise. The body needs time to warm up and increase the flow of blood and oxygen to the brain. Blood and oxygen are the fuels of the brain. If you remember something of physiology and anatomy, you will know that the muscles hold your organs in place and make it possible for them to perform their functions. I often visualize the organs of four-legged animals as being hung from their backbones like clothes from a line where they have been hung to dry. The animal finally stood on end and became man. Raise the clothesline on end and the clothes sag into a limp pile. Similarly, a person's organs would pile up at the bottom if there were not muscles to hold them in place. This is why someone who neglects himself physically will finally own a protruding abdomen, a prolapsed stomach, fallen bowels, or some other similar condition. Which brings us to the Burnout, Rust-out Theory: My mentor, Grandmaster Peter Urban, once said to me: "I would rather burn out than rust out!" What he meant was that he would rather keep physically fit than fall apart from non-use. Here are the Martial Arts of Motivation:

> Let's go! (Initiation Stage)
> Keep going! (The Life Process)
> There is nothing else! (Reality)

In gaining good health, we must first achieve a discipline. We must know in our minds that we want to improve our condition, and realizing this, we must conscientiously take the steps to achieve our goal. Keep at it, every day, a little at a time. Make it a part of your daily routine, a period well spent, and in short order you will see and feel the results of your improvement. In time, encouraged by these obvious gains, you will discover that you sincerely enjoy the exercise. And in due course (not as long as you might think), the effects of your discipline will become a reality. . . .

JUMPING ROPE

Start slowly. Remember for exercise to be beneficial, it should be both rhythmical and sustained, not stressful. Jumping rope takes a lot of concentration and coordination if it is to be done correctly. It is an excellent cardiovascular exercise—jumping rope makes the heart and lungs work harder. I recommend the alternate step to start, because the physical motion is similar to jogging. Jump only high enough to clear the rope. Keep relaxed and breathe normally.

The key components of smooth rope jumping are eye, hand, and foot coordination. It is good to jump initially without a rope, simulating the wrist and arm movements, keeping feet together while pushing off the balls of your feet. Your contact with the floor should not be heavy, but light, as in bouncing. You can do it in a small amount of time (research shows that 10 minutes of rope jumping equals 30 minutes of jogging in the area of cardiovascular efficiency). You can exercise the calves, thighs, abdomen, arms, chest, shoulders, back, heart, and lungs, all at the same time. The study of the martial arts is an exciting and fun way to good health.

In addition, the psycho-physical program in this book will help you to:

1. Develop coordination
2. Develop stamina (the "iron will")
3. Develop muscle strength and tone
4. Develop quickness and agility
5. Trim excess weight.

3. Hand Techniques
(Form and Practical Application)

Hand techniques are any technique applied with the hand, forearm, elbow, fist, and fingers. It is not necessary to callus your knuckles or any such craziness—proper techniques executed to a vulnerable area will be effective. You have used your hands since birth, so you have natural coordination. Start with a positive attitude. Your hands are naturally faster than your legs; leg techniques are much slower and harder to perfect, and should only be used when moving closer to your attacker. We call the distance between you and your attacker "critical distance." Stay out of range of attack until you formulate a plan of attack. And finally, never become one-sided—always practice techniques with both hands.

I teach fifty hand techniques, from beginner to black belt. Remember, you will always be able to use hand techniques. It is not the same with leg techniques, which depreciate with age. The Chinese Goju System uses 60 percent hand techniques and 40 percent leg techniques. Most kung fu systems are 80 percent hand techniques and 20 percent leg techniques (kung fu styles are not noted for powerful leg attacks). The hand techniques discussed in this chapter are the best of both worlds, karate and kung fu.

THE SUNFIST
(Rotary Punching)

1. The sunfist originated from Shaolin boxing (Chinese karate). It was sometimes referred to as the rocket punch because of the tremendous speed and power generated. Speed is equal to power; the faster the punch, the harder the impact force. Speed amplifies hit power. Shoulder-width stance is the starting position. Power is increased with mechanical precision synchronized with mental (high energy) input. Remember, true martial arts are 90 percent mental and 10 percent physical.

2. To start rotary punching, place both hands directly in front of you at shoulder height. The right hand should be placed at full extension, which is at chest height and centered above the left hand. The left hand is positioned near the base of the right elbow. After completion of the punch, each hand is placed alternately to the centerline position before extension of punching hand.

3. The shoulders should not move when punching. Keep your back erect. Punch directly in front of your chest, not in front of your shoulders. Punching from the centerline goes directly to the target with maximum muscle action. Centerline punching automatically blocks an opponent's punch without any wasted motion. Always punch with a target in mind. Be sensitive and alive; become your technique.

Supplementary Progressive Resistance

Progressive resistance is used to increase muscle density and stamina development. Proper muscle contraction aids in full-power delivery of technique. Weight training is an endurance-building exercise. Stamina drills increase the iron will or positive mental attitude—IRON WILL TRAINING.

A. Stand in a shoulder-width stance with elbows in and knees bent slightly. Relax and concentrate totally.

B. The right hand moves directly out at shoulder height to centerline punching position. NOTE: Left hand automatically moves to centerline for the next punch and protection.

C. As the left hand punches, the right hand retreats to centerline guard-and-strike position. Keep shoulders straight when punching. Also, extend the punching arm until the elbow locks.

D. The extending and retracting arm is aligned with the center of the body. Work at a fluid motion until the punch is perfected mechanically.

NOTE: In the centerline position, the perfect synchronization of punching, circular extension and retraction is maintained. The sunfist is the fastest and most effective punch in the Chinese Goju System. "Practice makes perfect."—RVC.

THE SUNFIST

STEP ONE: Shoulder-width stance.
Both arms in closed-fist chamber.
NOTE: Forearm parallel to ground—knees are not locked, legs are bent. Relax.

STEP TWO: Right sunfist punch at shoulder height.
Left hand is in chamber.
Snap the wrist upward as you strike.
NOTE: Centerline punch; chamber is like a compressed spring.

STEP THREE: Left sunfist punch at shoulder height.
As left hand punches, the right hand moves to chamber
NOTE: Centerline punch, punch with speed and power. Don't cheat on technique for speed.

STEP FOUR: Completion of exercise.
Back to original posture.
Always execute techniques correctly.
NOTE: Fist is relaxed until moment of contact.

Practical Application

A. Grab and punch to face are simultaneous with a forward motion.

B. Grab and punch to breathing system are simultaneous while moving forward.

THE TWIN SUNFIST

Form—Proper punch alignment without shoulder movement. Snap the elbows and wrist with speed. Punch, don't push.

NOTE: Executed from fighting stance. Use forward motion to amplify hit power.

Practical Application

A. Targets: chest and groin. NOTE: Best applied with sidestepping motion against frontal attack.

B. Targets: chin and stomach. NOTE: Commonly used in combination with kicking attacks. Sometimes followed with a sweep, throw, or take down.

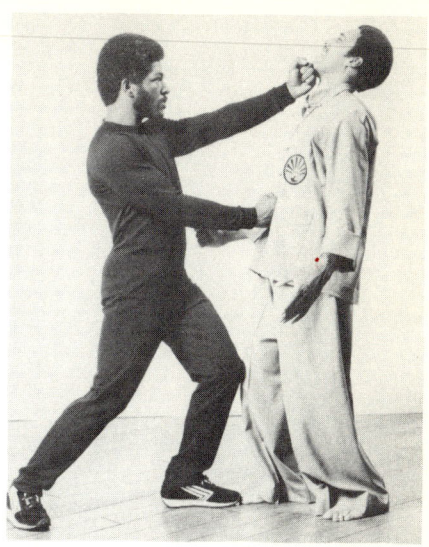

THE ELBOW STRIKE

STEP ONE: Shoulder-width stance with both hands in chamber position. Then execute the right elbow strike; opposite hand is in chamber. Note that the hands are open.

STEP TWO: Keep the arm that is striking parallel to the ground to complete the technique. Always execute techniques with both arms. As the left arm strikes, the right arm goes to chamber.

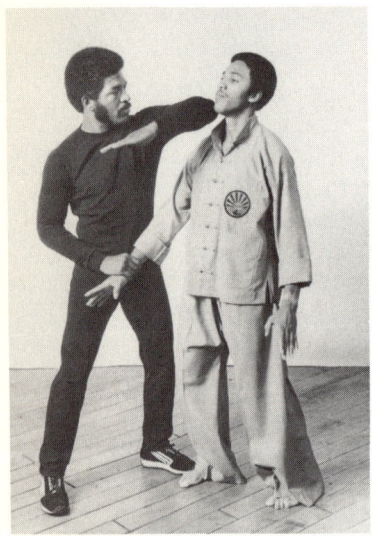

Practical Application

A. Best used with grab. Targets: chin, jaw, face, neck.

B. Sometimes used after ducking a face attack. Elbow strikes work well with knee attacks.

THE HOOK PUNCH

STEP ONE: Keep elbows close to body. Maintain shoulder-width stance. Relax and concentrate on correct execution of all techniques. Complete concentration is necessary to technique development.

STEP TWO: Use complete body motion. Keep elbow higher than fist for maximum effect. Total commitment with all technique.

Practical Application

A. The elbow, shoulder, hip, and leg work together. Hook power comes from snap action.

B. When using hook punch, keep opposite hand up to guard position. Hook works well with elbow follow-up. Punch, don't swing.

THE IRON PALM

The iron palm is a most effective weapon for self-defense. It is a combination strike and push, sometimes referred to as a "shock shove." This strike is basically a control device. The strike is made with the whole hand (palm and fingers). All hand techniques are practiced in the shoulder-width stance. Practice in slow motion until you have grasped the mechanical design.

1. The shoulder-width stance is designed to minimize physical stress in practice of Chinese Goju drills. Bend your legs and breathe normally. Both hands are placed in the chamber, palms facing up. (The chamber is the preparatory position for all basic hand techniques.) Always keep your forearms parallel to the floor. The chamber loosens up the shoulder and arm muscles.

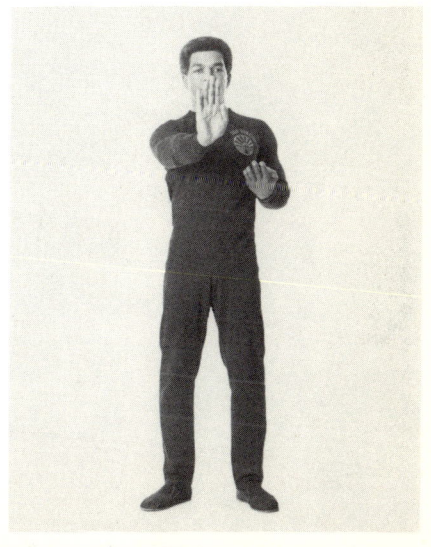

2. Extend your arm forward, making sure that the forearm slides against the side of your body. The finished position of the iron palm is when the hand is centered and at face height. Always keep your fingers straight, thumbs tucked in so as not to incur injury. Exhale as the hand is moving forward. Remember to center your technique. As the right hand retracts, the left hand starts its forward motion.

3. While the left hand is moved forward, the right hand goes to the rear, back to the chamber position. It is the coordination of forward and backward motion that amplifies the impact strike force. Remember, always relax. Make sure that all techniques are centered at completion stage.

Practical Application

A. When used to the chin, the iron palm affects the spinal cord through the neck. It can be used to the face, stomach, and/or groin, and works very well with the grab and pull devices. Always maintain a constant forward motion when executing any technique.

B. The ribcage is very vulnerable to the iron palm, especially if the arm is raised when striking. A chamber is not necessary to execute the iron palm. The power comes from the momentum created by body movement.

Important Factors: When using the iron palm, strike with the whole hand, not just the palm edge. The fingers and hand give a larger strike area, thus making it very effective. Put your whole body behind the initial shock and follow through. The iron palm works well with the tiger claw (described below).

THE MONKEY ELBOW

1. When grabbed from the rear, don't resist the force! Relax and concentrate on proper execution of technique.

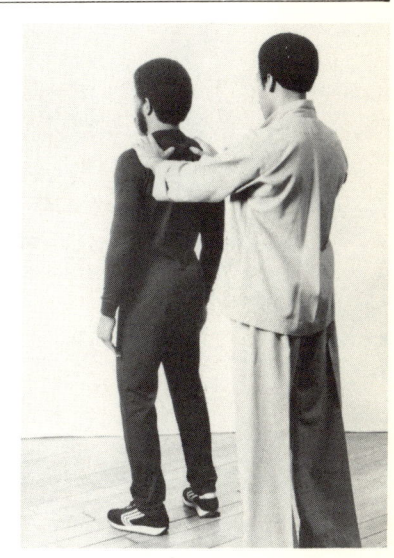

2. Step to your rear with elbow strike. It is not necessary to look at the attacker. Just react to the slightest touch—sensitivity and awareness are the key.

3. The right hand pushes the left arm to the rear with a thrusting motion. The target is the breathing system.

Application Against the Middle-Section Front Kick

A. The grab and the downward elbow are delivered together while executing a sidestep motion. NOTE: Grab is to back of leg.

B. The downward elbow should be to the knee or thigh muscle for optimum effect. NOTE: Grab is to the side of leg.

THE SNAKE FIST

There are fifteen different animal styles, the Snake being one of my favorites. Snake fist techniques come from the Chinese and Southeast Asian forms of martial arts. The snake is powerful, swift, and flexible. Emphasis is placed on total control of your opponent—movements of the snake are fluid power in motion. The snake attacks only the vital areas, such as the eyes, throat and sides and back of neck. There are a variety of choking and restricting techniques in the numerous snake forms; needless to say, there are very few kicking techniques. Remember, speed and accuracy are the key points.

I first encountered the Snake style in Hong Kong in the late 1960s. My good friend Jason Pai Piao introduced me to Sifu Leung Ting. *Sifu* is the Cantonese word meaning teacher; in ancient China, anyone who did anything well was considered a sifu. Sifu Leung Ting was an older gung fu brother of the "little dragon," Bruce Lee. From Sifu Leung Ting I learned the basics of the Wing Tsun style of gung fu. The movements of the crane and snake are woven into the Wing Tsun style. Wing Tsun is the most practical of the gung fu systems for self-defense. The style was created by a woman approximately two-hundred years ago; there are over seventy-five different forms of Chinese gung fu in existence today.

Remember, detail is important in the technical design of the Snake style. Be patient, and always relax when training.

THE SNAKE FIST

Snake fist techniques are practiced in the Chinese Goju shoulder-width stance. Spread your feet to the width of your shoulders and slightly bend your legs. Relax. This particular snake technique is called the white snake. Start out in slow motion. The fingers are not rigid until the point of contact. Remember to keep one of your hands in the guard position when striking with the opposite hand. Stay loose. Exhale as you strike, inhale as you retract your hand. Always practice techniques with the right and left hands.

Side View (right side)—Note the slight bend at the knees. Try to keep your back and shoulders aligned. Always keep fingers together and thumbs tucked to prevent self-injury.

Side View (left side)—Develop a flow with your technique. Be continuous and maintain the rear guard when executing any front hand technique.

Practical Application of the Snake Fist in Self-Defense

Defense against the front wrist grab. Don't resist the wrist grab, move directly forward with the snake fist to the throat.

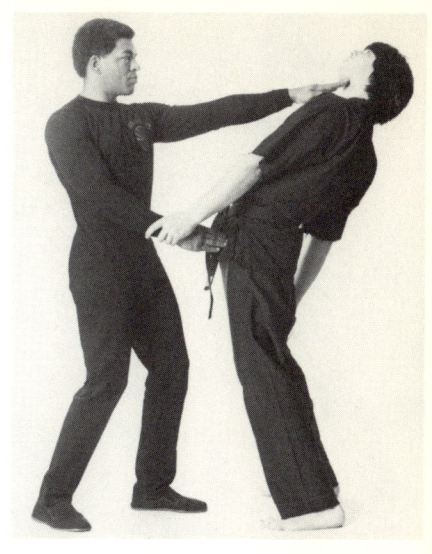

Snake Fist Attack and Control

A. Movements of the snake are not just hand movements but combinations of direct footwork supplementing rapid hand attacks. To the snake stylist, the eyes are very important as direction finders. The eyes gauge the distance between you and your opponent; your feet close the distance. Remember to remain outside the critical distance until you decide on your personal plan of action.

B. The left hand and foot are synchronized with the forward motion principle. Attack the eyes and grab your opponent's arm to increase control, which leads to technical accuracy. It is most important to be accurate in both offensive and defensive mechanisms. Remember to maintain a tight grab on your opponent's forearm. Notice that the forward motion is angular in position. It is best to be on the side that is not protected. Keep going!

C. After attacking eyes, the left hand moves downward in a slapping motion. At the same time, the right hand strikes the throat. The left hand grabs to immobolize your attacker's right hand. Remember to be in constant forward motion. Practice this first in slow motion, then at a fluid speed. Always attack the weak and unguarded areas of the body, e.g., the eyes, throat, groin, and sides and back of neck. Never stop your forward motion; even if you miss your target, continue. The snake is patient!

D. Always practice techniques with both arms to acquire a natural flow of technique. Continue the attack with the eye strike by the left hand. Sometimes you can try to execute both strikes to the eyes and the throat at the same time. Double-hand striking is a standard technique in the Chinese styles but is uncommon to the various karate styles.

The Snake Fist Attacks in Motion

A. Be creative! Maintain a natural, continuous flow when executing any martial arts techniques. NOTE: Wrist lock, knee strike, and eye attack all take place at the same time.

B. Use angular forward footwork to evade a front kick attack. Sidestep and counter with ankle grab coordinated with eye attack. Keep going! Snake fist techniques work very well with karate techniques.

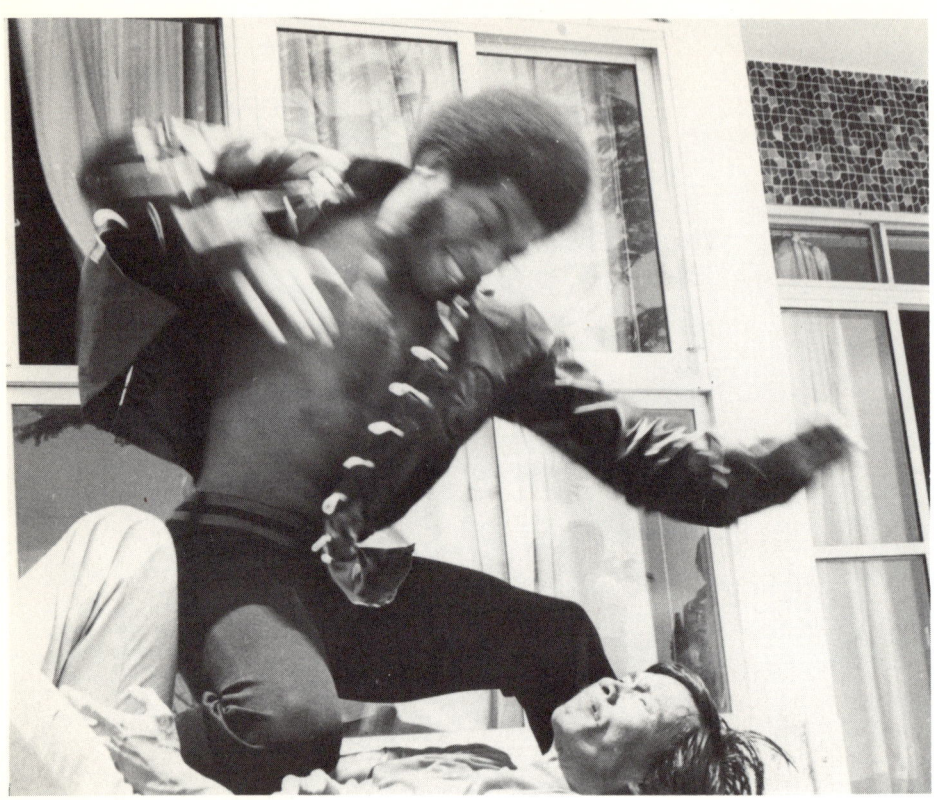

THE TIGER CLAW

Movements of the tiger combine ripping and tearing techniques with constant forward motion. The tiger is fierce in combat—the Chinese say: "Never disturb a sleeping tiger." I first saw the Tiger style in the early 1960s, in Chinatown in New York. Sifu Wai Hong of the Tiger-Claw School was demonstrating a prearranged set. I was impressed with the grace and technical proficiency of a "real" gung fu master. Form is what the karate people call kata and gung fu people call sets or forms. The terminology is different, but the feeling and technical expression stem from the same mental and physical output. Remember, the tiger maintains total control with the use of the palms and fingers. Movements of the tiger attack the throat, face, and groin area. The great masters of gung fu were capable of ripping bark off trees with their tiger claw techniques.

The Black Tiger of Shantung was a great kung fu disciple who had trained at the famous Shaolin Monastery in Canton, China. It is commonly believed that all forms of martial arts came from this monastery. About four thousand years ago, great gung fu masters documented the existence of the Black Tiger style. During this period, "death matches" determined the effectiveness of the various styles.

Remember that martial arts are a weapon. Always be careful in training; never strike the vital areas during a training session.

THE TIGER CLAW
(Movements of the Tiger)

1. All hand techniques of the Black Dragon Gung Fu System are practiced in the shoulder-width stance. This is a stationary drill. Always keep the elbows close to the body to protect the ribcage area; this also gives the forward motion additional spring. The tiger claw can be executed with one or both hands at the same time. Relax and concentrate all of your energy to your fingers and palms. The tiger claw works well with the iron palm technique in combination. First the palm, then the claw! Remember to exhale as your arms extend and inhale with the pulling motion.

2. Exhale through the mouth and inhale through the nose. Try to keep your shoulders and back straight. Concentrate your Chi (intrinsic energy) to the palms and fingers. The tiger claw is a ripping and tearing technique of the Black Tiger style.

3. Practice the tiger claw with both hands, then each hand separately. Maintain a constant flow of motion with emotional content. The result should be fierce and unrestricted in total mental and physical expression. Think like a tiger! When your mind and body become one, you can flow with the various movements of the tiger.

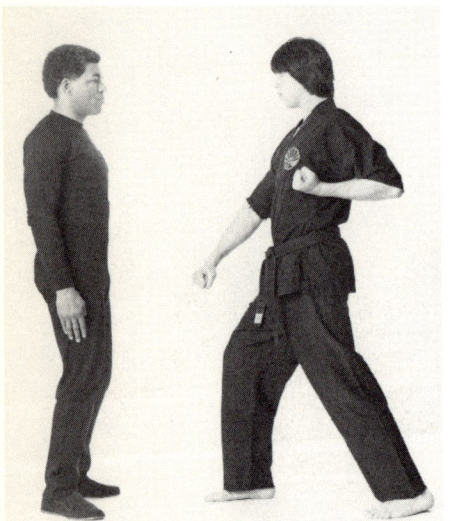

Practical Application of the Tiger Claw in Self-Defense Drill 1

A. This is one of the psycho-physical drills in the Chinese Goju System used to develop technical proficiency. Remember always to move toward your opponent; never back up. Backing up allows your opponent to gain momentum, and thus increases the force against you. Stick to your opponent like glue. Relax and concentrate on the attacker's initial move. Good eyes can detect offensive actions before actual physical contact. Always seize the opportunity!

B. Start your angular forward motion as your opponent starts the punching action. Your left hand goes directly to the throat with a tiger claw. At the same time, the right hand rips the left forearm. In the Chinese Goju System both hands are used simultaneously, one hand blocking and the other hand attacking. Eye, hand, and foot coordination is necessary to acquire complete technical ability. Remember, never stop your forward motion.

C. Continue the constant forward motion! Maintain a tight grip on the throat with the left hand. After releasing your opponent's left arm, execute a ripping technique to the back of the thigh. This technique creates high-intensity pain—ripping and tearing techniques attack the bio-computer (brain) and the structure of the body. It is possible to rip muscles, tendons, and ligaments, which causes permanent structural damage.

D. Continue the forward motion with a downward tiger claw to the face. Always strike with the palm, then tear with the fingers. Note how the forearm is in contact with the body. Maintain constant pressure with the forearm and elbows for total control. No matter what technique you use, make it work for you.

Practical Application of the Tiger Claw in Self-Defense Drill 2

A. Always make eye contact first (action and reaction). Remember the constant forward motion theory. As your attacker makes physical contact, you start your bio-computer. Relax and concentrate for total creative freedom.

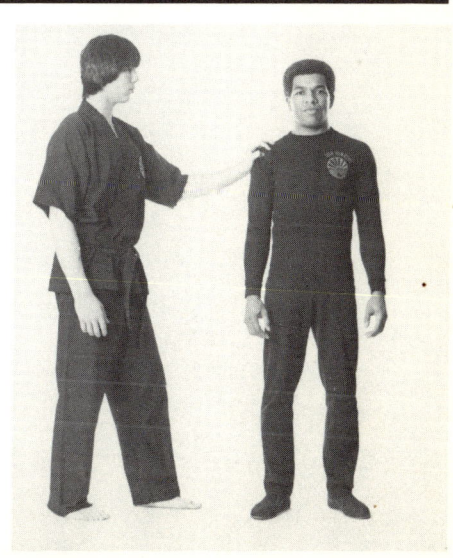

B. Pivot 90 degrees in the direction of your attacker. At the same time execute the double tiger claw to the neck, shoulder muscles, or chest in a forceful downward motion. Your hands and feet must work together! Concentrate on the ripping and tearing feelings. Remember to use your body weight to amplify the initial shock of impact.

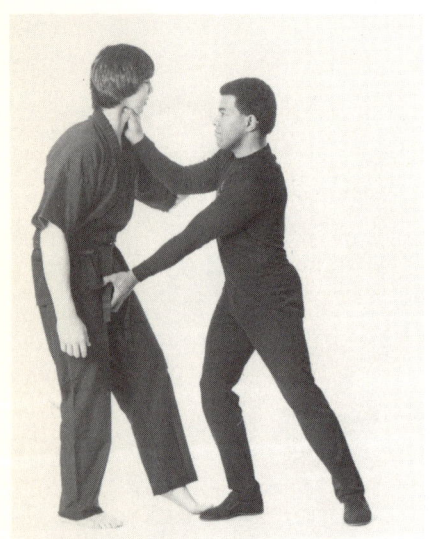

C. Follow through with a double tiger claw to the throat and groin area. Squeeze the throat with the fingers of the right hand and grab the groin area. Always maintain a constant forward motion when on the attack. Remember to practice the tiger claw with the emphasis on the palm and the fingers.

Practical Application of the Tiger Claw in Motion

Practice the movements of the tiger while moving forward—the forward motion amplifies the hit power tremendously. Note that one hand is high, the other low, to maintain total protection during the execution of all hand techniques of the tiger claw. If your left leg is forward, your left hand should be executing the tiger claw. Equally, when your right side is working, you must coordinate the right leg to react simultaneously.

MOVEMENTS OF THE TIGER

1. The movements of the tiger are incorporated into the Chinese Goju and Black Dragon Gung Fu systems. Note the aplication of the double tiger claws to the bio-computer and the groin area at the same time. Remember that mental attitude is just as important as technical proficiency. When moving forward with a double tiger claw, always keep shoulders and back straight. The elbow and arm and hand muscles add to the final effect of the technique.

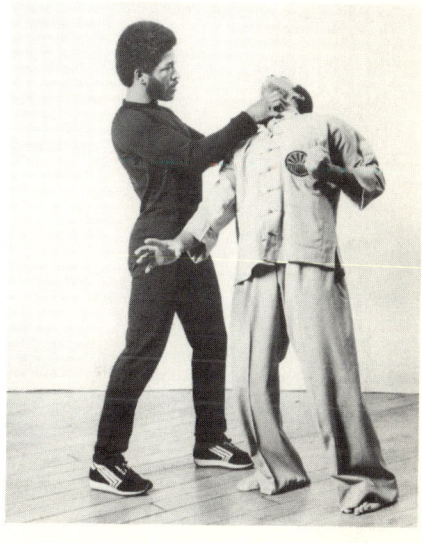

2. Choke the throat and rip the shoulder. Keep going! Use footwork to close the critical distance. Always stay as close as possible to your attacker to minimize his technical abilities.

3. Rip the throat and groin at the same time. Note the forward motion: be on the side of your attacker, not in front. The side forward motion uses the whole body to increase the total hit power. Hit power means the effectiveness of your technique!

4. Rip the eyes and attack the stomach at the same time. Coordination is the key factor in the proper execution of this technique. Try to be creative in executing the different applications of the tiger claw. Remember the laws of emotion and motion. Technical ability means freedom to experience the choice of technique fluency. All technique must flow like water!

5. Grab the throat and the groin area at the same time. Make sure that you have a tight grip on both areas of attack. Angular forward motion is crucial. Never waste any techniques; use only what has been tried and tested. A known quantity is a technique that is effective. Unknown quantities are fantasy technique and have not entered the world of reality.

6. Coordinate the tiger claw with a wrist grab to pull your opponent into the critical distance. Keep your forward motion fast and light. Never be rigid in motion. Techniques work if you have practiced sufficiently. Practice your hand techniques every day. Technical skills are not permanent; they must be maintained with daily practice. Remember, patience and practice are the golden rules of the martial arts.

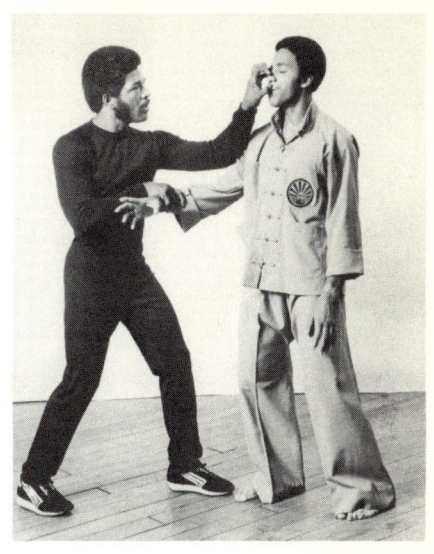

7. Bring your right forearm downward to the chest and grab the throat. Maintain constant forward pressure to increase the effectiveness of all your techniques. The Tiger style is a very effective form of gung fu for self-defense.

Points to remember:

    Constant Forward Theory
    Speed and flexibility
    Footwork
    Coordination of hand and eye
        range-finding devices

Chinese Goju is one of the few karate systems that employ animal forms and karate techniques to create an effective, harmonious blend of technique variables. I teach animal forms to white belt beginners and advanced Black Belts. Never waste any physical energy. Always let your technique flow like an electrical current.

4. The Black Dragon Blocking System (Form and Practical Application)

The Black Dragon Blocking System is a combination of blocking techniques coordinated with offensive hand techniques. Simply, the first rule of martial arts is "Don't get hit!" In most traditional forms of the arts, blocking is taught as an independent motion from attacking. The mechanisms of blocking and countering must be executed simultaneously for maximum effect. Imagine a street situation where you are hit in the head with an iron pipe. No matter how good your martial skills are, they are of no value, because you have been seriously injured first. So remember, *Don't get hit!* For optimum effect, soft blocks should be coordinated with hard hand techniques. The most common mistake made is to neglect effective blocking mechanisms.

Always try to relax, even in stressful situations. In general, most styles of martial arts are deficient in blocking technique training. You may be great when it comes to throwing techniques, but how are you at blocking hand and leg techniques with your face?

Blocking must be practiced daily to be maintained. The Black Dragon Blocking System is simple in concept and practical application. It should be practiced in front of a mirror or with a training partner; practice the blocking form in slow motion until technical proficiency is acquired. There are three types of speed in the martial arts: Slow motion is the learning speed; fluid motion is the practice speed; full speed is the maximum speed possible for each student in a life-and-death situation (reality).

Always relax and breathe normally when practicing any martial arts techniques. Remember, never cheat yourself when executing techniques!

FORM AND TECHNIQUE

Opening Posture—Right hand is clenched in a fist while the left hand is open with the fingers extended. The feet should be spread at shoulder width for central balance. The legs should be bent slightly for shock absorption. NOTE: Your ankles and knees are the shock absorbers. Relax and look directly in front of you.

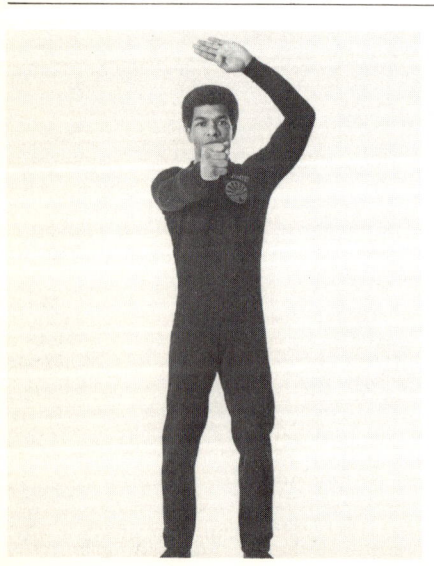

1. The left hand executes the rising block and the right hand executes the sunfist. Both hands are in the center of the body and aligned. A straight line could be drawn from the blocking hand through the punching hand and down to the belt level to ensure proper centerline position. The left hand is open and the right hand is closed. Block and punch simultaneously. The right hand executes the palm-up block before . . .

2. The right palm grabs as the left hand executes the iron palm strike. Note that the body always shifts in the direction of the strike force. The body shift is accomplished with toe and heel pivot action, not by picking up the feet as in stepping. Remember, body shifting evades attack and generates more instant strike force. Pivot back to original posture. Grab and palm together! Shift, don't step.

3. The left hand is closed and delivers a sunfist to the face as the right hand executes the low palm block. Remember the centerline rule! Instant strike force is increased by proper elbow and wrist action. Snap the elbow and wrist for proper technique extension. Keep shoulders straight. The strike and the block should be together. Breathing system: exhale with strikes and blocks; inhale between techniques.

4. The left hand executes the side palm block and the right hand delivers a sunfist to centerline target. NOTE: Sunfist has variable targets: face, chest, stomach. For best results, use high block with low attack, low block for high attacks. Relax, breathe, and concentrate. Move with a constant flowing motion to develop technique; speed will come after technique is refined through proper practice.

5. The right palm-up block and left hand move to centerline guard position. The palm-up block stops the attack as the guard hand executes the counter. NOTE: The palm-up block (sometimes referred to as the slap block) is a defensive mechanism against upper- and middle-section attacks. This block is also a throat or eye attack when necessary. Finger jab to centerline.

6. The right hand grabs as the body pivots into left sunfist to face target. This shift is the same as the second movement of this exercise. Always shift in the same direction as your strike force. Remember to look in the direction of your attacks! Always be aware when practicing the Black Dragon Blocking System. Remain loose, hard, and fast. RELAX.

NOTE: The Black Dragon Blocking System can be practiced in various methods, with or without a partner. Advanced students develop all techniques on the wooden man. Important factors are:

> Breath control
> Footwork
> Blocking
> Attacking

Economy of motion—executing the correct technique without wasting time and energy. Whenever possible, observe proper form in technique delivery.

"Plan your work, work your plan!"—RVC

THE BLACK DRAGON BLOCKING SYSTEM
Practical Application: Part 1
Application of rising block with sunfist

A. **Ready Posture:** Immediate eye contact and a relaxed body. The back is straight. Feet are spread to a shoulder-width stance; keep legs slightly bent.

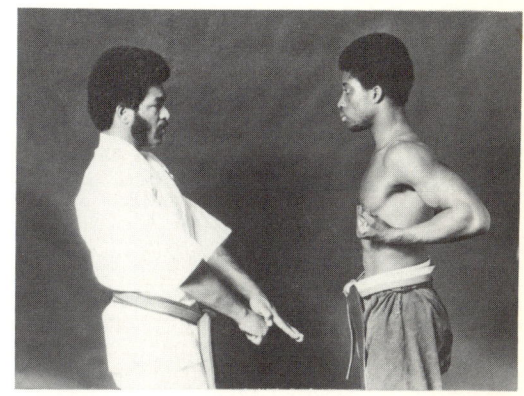

B. **Initiation Phase:** The block and punch start at the same time. Notice the blocking arm is parallel to the ground when making initial contact with attacker's arm. At this time, footwork is applied to increase the strike force when moving forward with attacks.

C. **Maximum Effort Phase:** The rising arm deflects the punch upward as the opposite hand delivers the sunfist to the middle or low target. It is a general rule to step forward with the same side, punching to generate more instant strike force. The assistance of the lower torso, particularly the hip and knee action, creates perpetual forward motion.

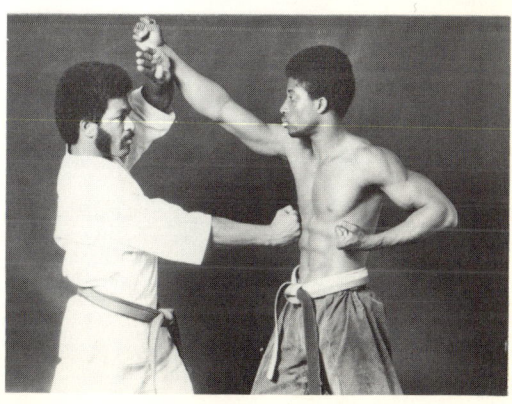

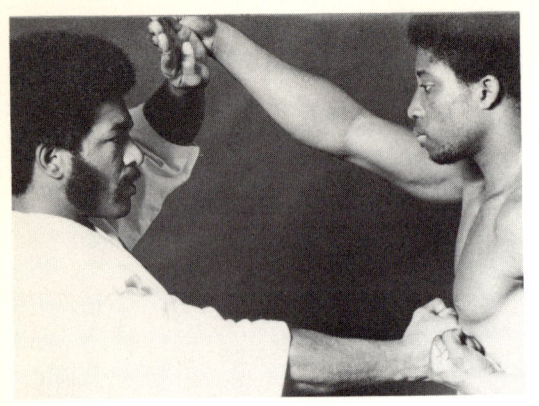

D. Evaluation and Analysis Phase: Van Clief's Law: Speed + Timing + Focus = ME (Maximum Effort). Remember the Creation of Force Principle: human engineering is the use of the complete body with limitless human potential (e.g., hip, leg, arm, and back action). NEVER BACK UP!

Practical Application: Part 2

Application of palm-up block with iron palm strike

A. Ready Posture: Always look at your opponent. You can't block what you can't see. Relax, and try to sense your attacker's initial attack before it develops.

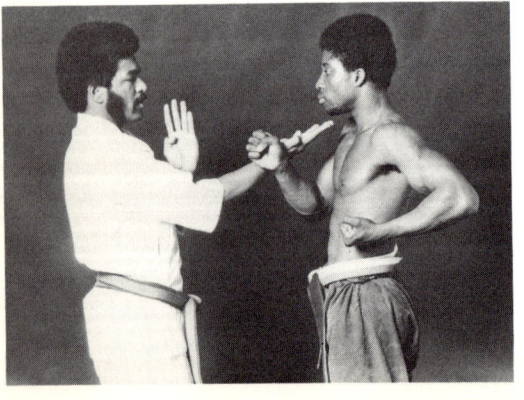

B. Initial Contact Phase: Reach out with your block to stop the attacking arm. Notice opposite hand is in guard position. The palm-up block must strike the attacking arm in a downward motion. Remember the centerline principle.

C. **Follow-Up Phase:** Continue the downward motion of the palm-up block to expose the upper torso to counterattack. Start your forward motion in preparation for the iron palm strike to face or neck target. Shifting the body forward evades the punch and increases counterattack variables.

D. **Maximum Effort Phase:** Snap the left iron palm to the face as you pull down with the grab to intensify the instant strike force. Maintain a constant forward motion (CFM) while delivering all technique. The attack must be an explosion of mechanical and spiritual expression.

E. **Variation:** Note that important factors are speed, proper technique, positive mental attitude (PMA). Always protect your centerline and develop technique flow. Keep going! Never back up.

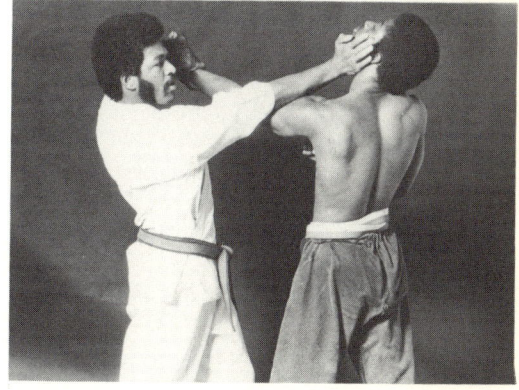

Practical Application: Part 3

Application of low palm-up block
with upper sunfist strike

A. Natural Body Position: Always relax and never anticipate moves. Eye contact means the ability to evaluate and analyze the complete situation. Important factors: pattern recognition, classification, human engineering, creative imagination.

B. Maximum Effort Phase: As the attacker moves forward with the low-area punch, execute a right low palm to the attacker's wrist or forearm while executing the left sunfist punch to the face area. The block and the punch should be considered one movement. Remember to snap your wrists and elbows to full extension.

C. **Evaluation and Analysis Phase:** Shoulders are straight and back erect. Make sure of proper block and counter centerline alignment. Never waste motion! Exhale as you block and counter as a general rule. NOTE: Thumbs are bent for protection.

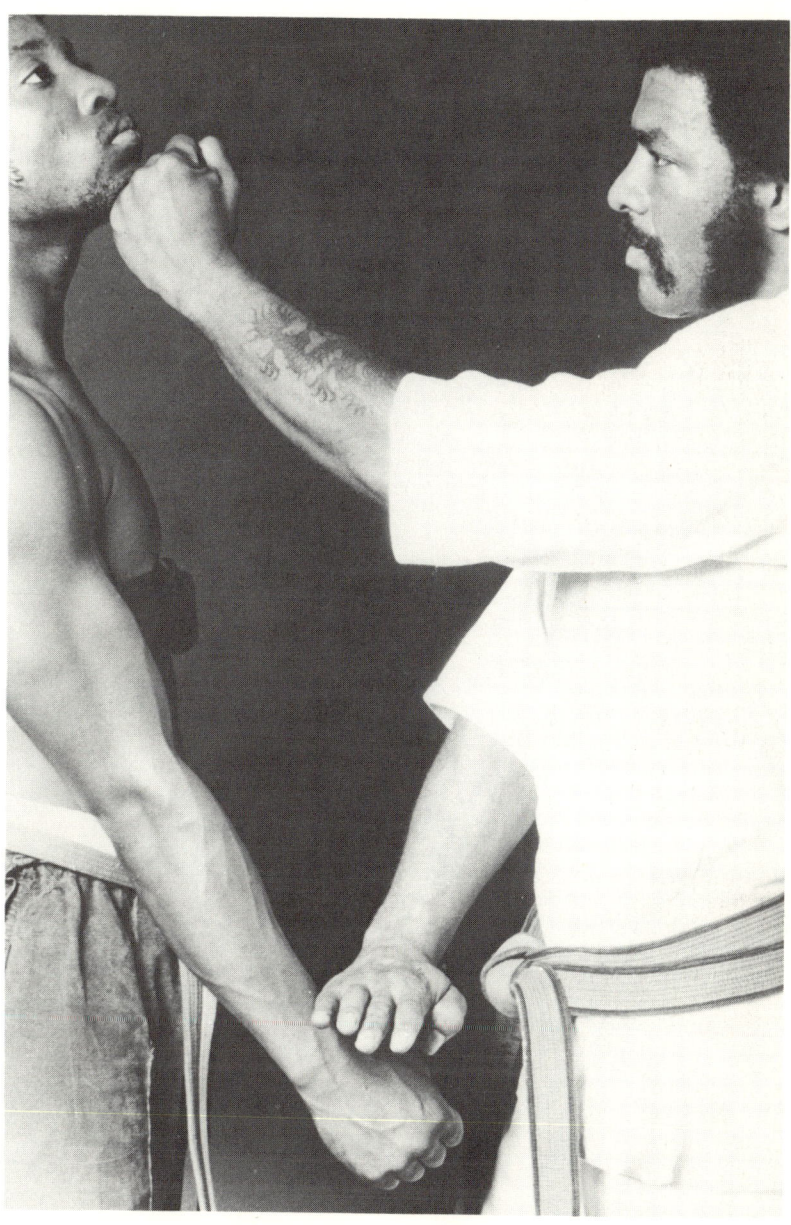

NOTE: Hand positions are interchangeable (blocks and counters can be applied simultaneously with either hand). Always commit yourself fully with your technique.

Practical Application: Part 4

Application of the side palm block
with middle sunfist punch

A. **Ready Posture:** Remember the critical distance—the range at which your attacker can hit you with hand or foot. Stay outside the critical distance until you evaluate the situation. Always be aware!

B. **Initiation Phase:** Move in! The side palm block is most effective against upper body attacks (chest and face). As your opponent extends his arm, maintain good defensive posture with a constant forward motion. Let your opponent commit himself. At this point, he is most vulnerable—don't back up!

C. **Contact Phase:** Timing is a very important factor in counterattacking. The purpose of open hand blocking is to deflect attacks. Open-hand blocks are soft blocks. Block soft and hit hard. Notice the rear hand is held high to protect the face while the opposite hand is low to guard the lower areas. As contact is made, shift body into the body punch to generate power.

D. **Maximum Effort Phase:** As you deflect the attacking punch to the outside of your body, commit yourself totally to counterattacking the exposed area. The breathing system attack is the best counter for the upper body assaults. Proper footwork with counterattacks minimizes the risk and increases the safety factor.

NOTE: Proper form in execution of technique is essential. The palm block can easily be connected to a grab for maximum control of your opponent. Always maintain technique flow to keep your opponent off balance. Never rush yourself! Keep good training habits.

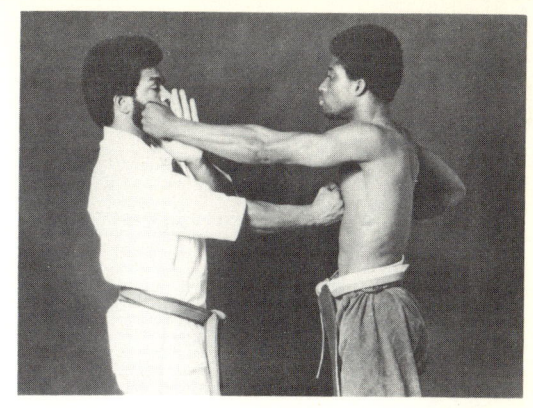

Practical Application: Part 5

Application of the palm-up block against upper body punching

A. **Ready Posture:** Remember to keep your guard up. It is best for your attacker to hit your arms instead of a vital area, e.g., face or breathing system. The best defense is a good offense—always press your attacker! Keep elbows in to protect the stomach and ribcage area. Relax, and wait for the correct moment to explode with technique.

B. **Contact Phase:** The palm-up block—sometimes referred to as the reverse slapping block—is generally applied with the arm that is closest to your attacker. The shock of the block is combined with a constant forward pressure on the attacking arm. This block is actually an attacking device. The constant pressure created temporarily traps your attacker's arm, which exposes his upper body to counterattack. Remember to reach out with this block.

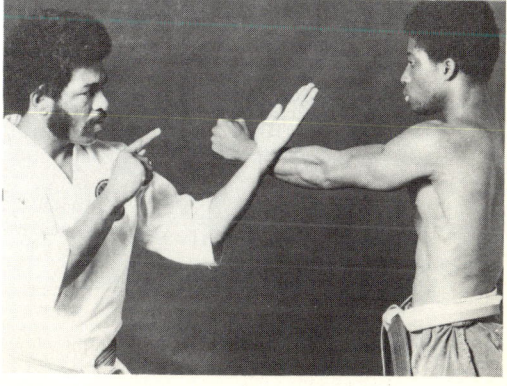

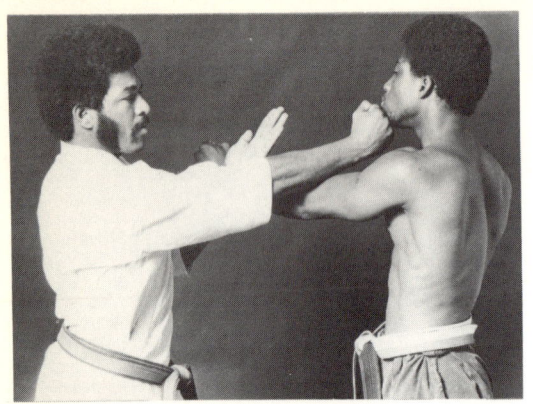

C. **Maximum Effort Phase:** The block and counter are applied at the same time, although the actual block is a split second before the punch. The power in the sunfist punch comes from the constant foward motion of the body with the punch. As this is the maximum effort phase, combine the positive mental attitude (PMA) with the proper technique for increased instant strike force (ISF). Let your techniques explode with energy!

D. **Reverse Angle:** Sometimes the palm-up block is applied with the inside arm instead of the outside arm. Under actual combat conditions, keep constant pressure on your opponent for best results. There are no general rules of combat, except to maintain a constant flow of technique at your opponent. Keep going until you defeat the attacker. Always have a positive mental attitude and never back up. Side step, body shift for optimum effect. Be flexible!

E. **Constant Forward Motion (CFM):** Important factors are:
    Body positioning (maximum control)
    Mechanical momentum (follow-through)
    Footwork (raised heel)
    Total commitment (maximum effort)
    Technical perfection

Practical Application: Part 6
Application of palm-up block and grab with sunfist attack

A. Sunfist punch to neck or chin with maximum snapping motion. The palm-up block is used to deflect attacks to the face and chest areas. Slap the attacking arm with the back of your open hand, making sure to tuck in the thumb to avoid injury. Rule 1: Don't injure yourself by improper techniques.

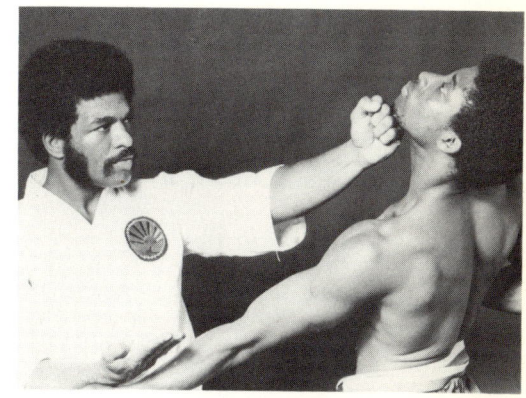

B. As soon as you slap the arm, immediately grab to ensure complete control. The grab increases the instant strike force when combined with a pulling motion. Pull your attacker in the direction of the striking force. At this time, the ideal follow-up technique would be an elbow strike with the the same hand that executed the sunfist punch. CTF (Constant Technique Flow).

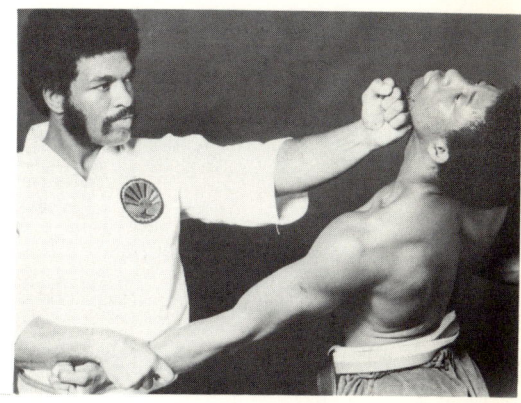

C. The punch is more devastating with the pulling action! Notice the position of the arm being pulled. At this point, you can block your attacker's counter- or potential counterattack with his own arm (trapping hands). It is ideal to strike the neck, chin, or jaw with the sunfist in an upward snapping motion. Always keep your eyes on your attacker. When punching, punch—don't push! Keep good training habits. Remember that grabbing techniques are control mechanisms. Example: grab/punch and grab/kick devices.

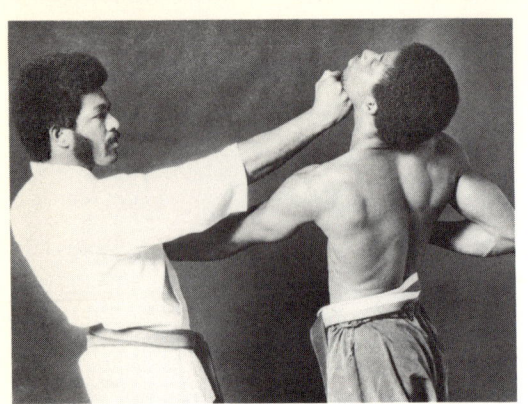

D. Important factors are:
 Wrist and arm projection (elbow action)
 Shoulder motion and back erection
 Hip and suspension system synchronization (footwork)

Van Clief's Law of INSTANT STRIKE FORCE (Hit Power)

Snap + Whip + Positioning = Maximum Punching Power
(arm)   (body)   (footwork)

(Relax until the moment of impact)

5. Leg Techniques (Form and Practical Application)

Leg techniques are much harder to execute and to maintain at a proficient level; however, there are many advantages in leg-attacking mechanisms. It is my belief that leg techniques should be used only when closing distance or if an opponent moves out of hand range. Styles that tend to have more than 50 percent hand techniques are not really applicable to the life of the martial artist. Some of the Korean forms of the martial arts are not, in fact, very practical. Most Korean styles, such as Tae Kwon Do, Moo Duk Kwan, and Tang Soo Do, are imbalanced. To be realistic, a form should incorporate more hand techniques than leg techniques. Remember, our bodies are continually changing! Of course, there are special individuals who excel in kicking techniques—champions like Bill Wallace have mastered these techniques after years of constant practice.

Kicking can be a great asset to your personal arsenal if taught and practiced properly, but it is extremely hard to maintain one's kicking abilities. Very few people can execute high-kicking techniques with power. It is most efficient to kick to the lower area because low kicks are harder to block. Hands and legs should work together to cover the full range of your opponent's body. Hands work best when applied to the groin area and upward. The legs work best when applied to the stomach area and downward to the suspension system (the hips, legs, and feet).

Remember, always warm up before starting kicking drills. It is most important to keep your hands up in a guard position when executing these techniques. Never extend your kick fully with full speed; knee injuries are to be avoided. Always kick something! Kicking pads or heavy bags are good training aids. Kicking techniques should be practiced for three to four days at a stretch to achieve satisfactory results.

Bruce Lee, whom I met in the early 1960s, believed that kicking techniques should only be used when closing the distance. It was during this period that I first became interested in the Chinese martial arts. Bruce introduced me to the Wing Tsun style of kung fu. I will always remember Bruce; he was a friend and martial arts brother. Although Wing Tsun is 90 percent hand techniques, the kicking techniques are devastating. Most kung fu styles specialize in various low-area kicking attacks. It is up to you as the student to select the techniques of your choice. Whether they work is the bottom line! Be patient and always relax.

THE FRONT HEEL KICK

1. The shoulder-width stance is the Chinese Goju standard for all hand- and leg-technique drills. Your legs are spread apart to shoulder-width position, with knees bent for shock absorption. Notice arm positioning; the elbows are in, protecting your body. Fists are clenched and relaxed.

2. The chamber position is the preparatory position for all kicking. As the knee rises, the supporting leg is bent for balance and shock absorption. Pull your toes up in preparation for the downward snapping action. Kicking power is the combination of the hip, knee, and thigh coordinations.

3. Remember to keep the supporting leg bent for balance. Keep your back erect while kicking. The strike is made with the heel or the bottom of the foot, whichever is most comfortable. Hands do not move while kicking! This kick is never applied above groin height.

4. Always bring leg back to chamber after kicking. Proper chambering allows for combination kicking. Remember that hands do not drop while executing kicking maneuvers. The front heel kick can be delivered as a thrust or a snap kick. Example: Thrust kick—sledgehammer; snap kick—whip action.

5. Place the kicking leg back to the original position in preparation for opposite-leg kicking action. Practice all kicks with both legs. Start with the right leg, then the left. Begin slowly to develop proper mechanical execution. Never start at maximum speed!

NOTE: Keep in mind that kicking above groin height is very dangerous. The front heel kick is an excellent counterattack or defense against any kick above the waist. When your upper body is being attacked by a high kick, counter by kicking the supporting leg of your opponent. The groin, thigh, knee, and shin are the targets because they are difficult to protect.

Variations in Practical Application

A. Attacking mechanisms low-medium-high for maximum effect. This is an advanced form of Black Dragon Gung Fu. Blocking + kicking + punching = complete mechanical utilization. Note the wrist lever applied in combination.

B. Grab the wrist and attack the suspension system at the same time. Prepare to deliver a face punch with the right hand as the right foot is lowered.

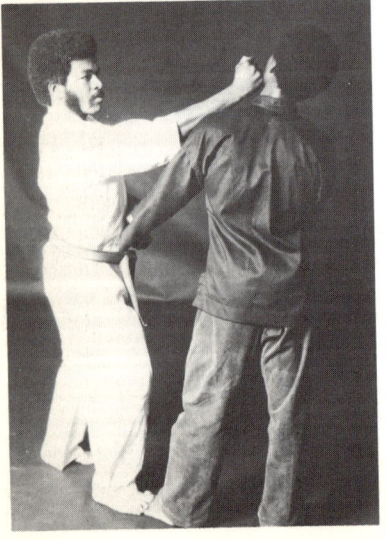

C. Jerk your attacker into the sunfist to increase the instant strike force potential. Always keep your eyes on your opponent.

D. As soon as your hand starts to retract to centerline, attack the suspension system again with your opposite leg. Practice kicking with both legs!

NOTE: Photographs B, C, and D are the combination of grabbing and kicking, when moving in a forward motion with hand techniques. Inertia is constant amplification of hit power with perpetual motion (constant motion principle).

THE LOW ROUND (INSTEP OR SHIN) KICK

Leg Attacks

1. Starting Position: the shoulder-width stance, with elbows in protecting the middle section. Relax and bend both legs for maximum support and balance. Remember your stance must never be wider than your shoulder width. Wide stances are dangerous!

2. As your right leg rises to the chamber position, both hands remain in guard position. Notice the toes of the chambered leg are pointed down. The chamber also guards the groin area. Keep the supporting leg bent for balance and shock absorption. Proper chamber action increases hit power.

3. Rotate the hip and leg forward at the same time as the pivoting action of the supporting leg. The supporting leg is most important in generating maximum effort kicking. Pivot on the ball of the foot and rotate the heel in the same direction as the kick force line.

4. Notice that the hands do not drop, as that would expose the upper body to attack. The kicking action must be like a whip snapping. Keep the toes pointed down throughout the entire kicking action. Kick with determination. Remember: Motion + Emotion = ME (high energy input).

5. Bring the kicking leg back to the chamber position to complete the kicking action. Remember, you are your technique! All techniques are alive and full of energy. Kicking action must extend and retract in one complete fluid motion. Slow kicking is self-destructive.

6. Place, not drop, your right leg back to the original starting position. Practice this technique at least 10 times on each leg. To change to the opposite side, just move your left leg to the rear and start again. Practice kicking with both legs regularly.

Practical Application of the Low Round Kick

A. Set your opponent up! Start your forward motion and attack the leg that is closest to you. Look into his eyes so as not to telegraph your intentions. Use a grabbing technique whenever possible.

B. The grab and the kick are executed at the same time. Kick his thigh, knee, or calf to upset his balance. At all times, keep your guard up. Never expose yourself to attack!

C. Continue your constant forward motion by delivering a front heel kick and sunfist with a grab and pull technique. All three techniques should be delivered at the same time for maximum effectiveness. Chinese Goju stresses total body control.

Important Factors:

1. Practice all techniques with correct form.
2. Never drop your guard.
3. Leg techniques are used to close the distance between you and your target.
4. Low kicks are best—to groin, thigh, knee, calf, and ankle.
5. Kicking techniques are hard to master. They must be practiced more than hand strikes to achieve reasonable proficiency. Kicking with accuracy and power requires constant practice.

THE MONKEY KNEE

The monkey knee is a favorite among Chinese Goju stylists. In an actual street situation, the distance between you and your attacker is quite close—normally all the action takes place within 3 to 4 feet. In 1974, I was in Hong Kong on location filming *The Black Dragon's Revenge*. My sifu, Leung Ting, introduced me to Grandmaster Chan Chou, "the Monkey King." Sifu Chan Chou has trained many kung fu superstars who are famous in the United States, such as Chan Goon Tai and Jason Pai Piao. When I visited the famous Shaw Brothers Studio, I met Bruce Lee's mentor. Director Chiang Cheh was responsible for two of Lee's early films, *The Big Boss* and *Fist of Fury*. Chiang Cheh is the Alfred Hitchcock of Hong Kong! I found him quite interesting.

Chan Goon Tai, who is an exponent of the Monkey style of gung fu, and won the All Asian Full Contact Championship in Taiwan, was completing a film entitled *The Iron Monkey*. The martial arts choreography was really unbelievable!

In Hong Kong there are over two thousand schools of the martial arts. The most popular forms of gung fu are Wing Tsun, Hung Gar, White Crane, Monkey, Eagle Claw, and Pak Mei (the White Eyebrow). In September of 1974 I was appointed U.S. representative for the Chung Wah Martial Arts Association in Hong Kong and shortly afterward I was elected director of gung fu studies of the United States. President Chan awarded me a lifetime membership in the Chinese Martial Arts Association of Hong Kong. My experiences with the Monkey style have been of great spiritual benefit to me. The "spiritual monkey" is one of the Shaolin temple styles of gung fu. "Practice makes perfect!"

THE MONKEY KNEE

1. The shoulder-width stance is the standard posture for executing all Chinese Goju techniques for beginners. Relax and breathe normally. Remember to keep legs slightly bent and always keep elbows close to the body. Try to keep both hands in a guard position when executing leg techniques. The most common bad habit of martial artists is to leave the head unprotected when delivering kicking attacks. Never let your hands drop; it is an invitation to get hit in the bio-computer. Keep those hands up at all costs! Close your fists without tension. Stand erect and look directly to your front.

2. Bring your right knee up to the level of your belt. Start slowly, only increasing speed after the basic mechanics are understood. It is the speed, not the power, of this technique that makes it effective. Bend the left leg slightly to maintain balance. Remember not to drop your hands throughout this kicking drill.

3. As you lower your right leg to the floor, raise the left knee to the level of your belt. It will be difficult at first to maintain your balance, but be patient. Practice the monkey knee in a flowing motion. Remember always to keep your hands in the guard position when delivering kicking attacks.

4. Side Angle—Note the slight bend in the left leg to help maintain balance. The toes of the right foot are pointed directly downward to the floor. Pulling the foot to the parallel position puts stress and tension on the foot and calf muscles. This tension slows down the forward motion of the foot. Relax your shoulders and fists. Remember to develop a constant fluid motion when executing this technique. If the technique is used correctly, your opponent won't even see it!

Practical Application of the Monkey Knee in Self-Defense

A. Sometimes you will have to react without seeing your attacker. This is a drill to prepare you for that time. Confrontation therapy is the code name for reality! Relax and breathe normally. Learn to react to your senses. Be aware!

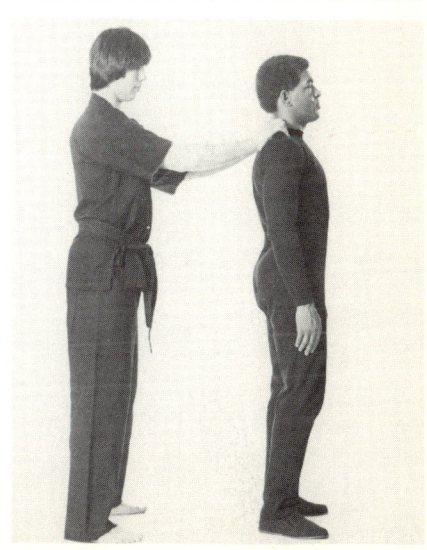

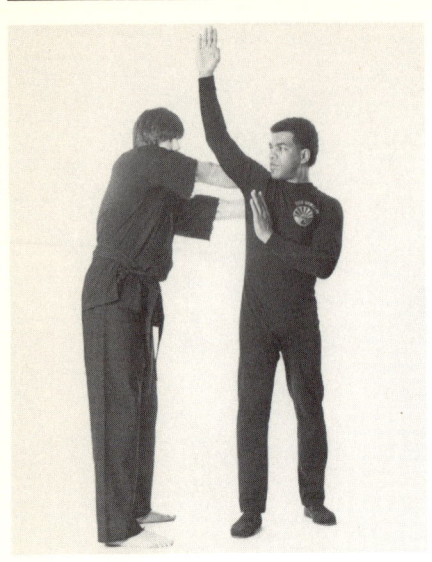

B. Always move in the direction of your attacker. Your right leg drops back to a position of shoulder width. At the same time your right arm starts to circle both of your attacker's arms. This technique derives from the Snake style of gung fu. Your left hand goes directly to the guard position.

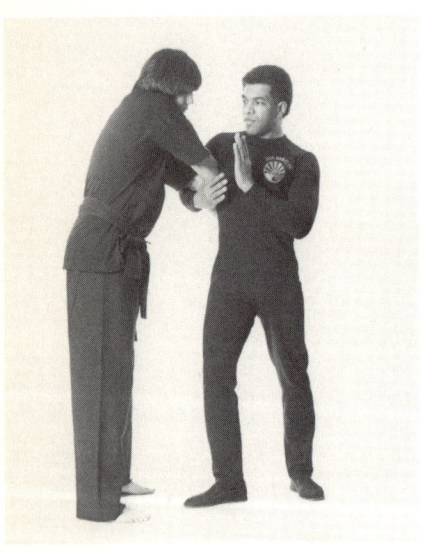

C. The right hand executes the coiling snake technique, your forearm wrapping around both of the attacker's arms. Try to bring your arm as close to you as possible. The coiling snake maintains a tight hold on both arms. Maintain the tightest grip you can. Remember, constant total pressure brings total control. Start to pull your attacker in your direction in preparation for your next technique. Let's go! Keep going! There is nothing else!

You control your attacker with the bicep and forearm lever. The coiling snake is a form of "trapping hands," a famous Wing Tsun technique. My first experience with trapping hands was with Bruce Lee, who was an expert in "chi sao," the Wing Tsun hand and foot sensitivity drill. The trapping hands technique would allow total control with total offense capabilities.

D. Now that you are in total control of your attacker, use the monkey knee to the lower abdomen or groin area. Always keep your toes facing the floor when delivering the monkey elbow. The "Thai boxers" are masters of the knee technique. The tightness of your hold, combined with the upward thrust of your body, increases the hit power potential. Remember always to keep your toes facing downward when delivering the monkey knee. The monkey knee should be practiced at least 20 times per training session.

THE FRONT KICK

1. Starting Position: The shoulder-width stance with legs slightly bent. Relax and breathe normally. Always keep your hands in the guard position. Then visualize in your mind's eye what the technique looks like. The front kick is used against an opponent's frontal attack; it may also be used to close the "gap." Kicks are primarily used to close the distance so that hand techniques can be used to finish off your opponent.

2. Bring your right leg up to the chamber position, remembering never to drop your hands from the guard position. Always bend your supporting leg to maintain balance when kicking. Keep elbows close to sides for protection and offensive mechanisms. Inhale as you start to bring your leg to chamber. Shift your body weight to center on the supporting leg. Don't tense up! It is common to lose your balance when practicing these drills. The practice of bringing the leg to chamber loosens the leg, hip, and stomach muscles. The chamber is a necessary component of all kicking techniques.

3. Slowly extend your right leg to centerline position. Make sure that you do not straighten the supporting leg when executing any kicking mechanisms. Always practice kicking techniques in slow motion until technical ability is acquired. The chamber position pushes the foot forward with increased speed and power. Always bring your leg back to the chamber position after completing any kicking techniques. The shin and foot protect the suspension system from attack when you kick.

4. Side View—Note that the striking surface is the ball of the foot. This kick should be practiced to the middle and low areas for maximum efficiency. Keep your hands in the guard position when executing any hand or leg techniques.

5. Side View—Always bring your kicking leg back to the chamber position. The chamber position enables the Chinese Goju student to deliver 12 different kicking maneuvers easily from the same chamber. Always relax and breathe normally.

Practical Application of the Front Kick in Self-Defense

A. Start the bio-computer! Relax and breathe normally. Let's go! Keep going! There is nothing else! Immediately make eye contact to analyze the situation and variables. In self-defense it is the speed of the reaction that is of utmost importance. Speed is equal to power!

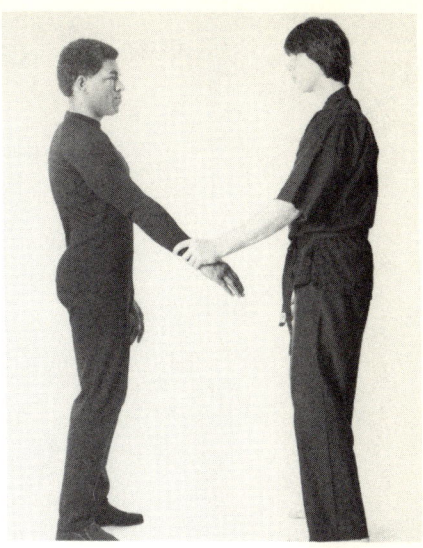

B. Without resisting the wrist grab, bring your right leg directly to chamber. Maintain eye contact throughout this self-defense training. Remember, if you can't see it, you can't block it.

C. Your leg must shoot forward to the target area without hesitation. The chamber is the cocking position for all leg techniques in the Chinese Goju System. Remember to escape the wrist grab by pulling your elbows in and pulling your forearms toward you. This maneuver is an aiki jitsu technique—aiki jitsu being the art of the Ninja. The Ninja were the intelligence agents of early Japan, trained in the martial arts of karate and aiki jistu. The Ninja were the "invisible assassins," commissioned by the feudal warlords for secret missions. We call aiki jitsu "escape and evasion" training. The internal rotation of the hands creates a lever on the attacker's thumbs. The pain is so intense that the attacker must let go of your wrists.

After you break the grab, continue the counterattack with the double tiger claw technique. The front kick works best when applied to the middle and low sections of the body. Remember, the toes are pulled back for protection of the kicking foot. In the street you will have on shoes or sneakers to protect the toes. When you kick, fully commit your hips, legs, and foot in a constant flowing motion. There are two types of kick: the snap kick and the thrust kick. The snap kick is used like a jab. The thrust kick is the power technique. Snap and thrust kicks serve the same purpose. Remember to use only what works for you!

THE SIDE KICK

The side kick is used primarily in karate forms, such as Tae Kwon Do, Shotokan, Kempo, Shorin-ryu, and Okinawa Goju. I can personally attest to the validity of the side kick as being most effective. During the early 1960s, champions like Joe Lewis, Louis Delgado, and Toyotaro Miyazaki became national and international grand champions because of their effective side kicks.

The side kick can be used as both an offensive and a defensive mechanism. The side thrust kick is much stronger than the side snap kick. Always keep your hands up when delivering kicking techniques, and always practice kicking with both legs to achieve a natural body flow. The Reverend Ronald Taganashi of the Zen Karate Clan had the best flying side kick I have ever seen. He could deliver the flying side kick in the street or ring with maximum effectiveness.

Master Taganashi is a master Ninja, who teaches fifty different Oriental weapons. I studied the art of Japanese Goju with him for about three years. He was an excellent kataman and could spar quite well; I once saw Taganashi kick his opponent out of the ring at a karate tournament. I believe his power comes from his strong spiritual and mental commitments to zen and the martial arts. Master Taganashi was a great inspiration to me in my formative years—I shall always remember the days of the 1,000 side kicks with Taganashi!

THE SIDE KICK

1. The opening posture is the side shoulder-width stance. Your body is at a right angle to your target. Line your shoulder up with the target. Remember always to keep your hands in the guard position while delivering kicking techniques. Look in the direction of your target, but not directly at it, so as not to telegraph your movements in advance. Relax and breathe normally. Think first, then react.

2. Bring your right leg directly into chamber. Keep your eyes on your attacker. Pull the chamber tight to protect your suspension system. Note the bend in the right leg for balance.

3. Slowly extend your leg in alignment with the shoulder line to the target. Always practice kicking techniques in slow motion so as not to incur self-injury. The heel and the bottom of the foot are the ideal surfaces for contact against the human body. Some styles use the blade of the foot to kick with. I don't recommend this as an effective method of side kicking—the blade is not as strong as the heel, nor as durable. Keep your hands up.

4. Always bring the kicking leg back to chamber before lowering to the floor. Make sure your knee is at the level of your belt. Inhale as you chamber, exhale with delivery.

5. The finish position is the side shoulder-width stance. Keep your elbows as close to your body as possible. I recommend 10 to 15 repetitions of the side kick on each side every day. This is how the side kick is practiced at a training session. First in slow motion, then at fluid speed.

Practical Application of the Side Kick

A. Pick out your target and align your body. Keep out of range until you have a plan; then take advantage of every opportunity.

B. Close the gap with a grab. Start the cocking (chamber) action with a rear cross step moving forward. Keep supporting leg bent.

C. Always keep your eyes on your opponent. Concentrate on proper heel thrust while moving forward. The grab works very well with the side (thrust) kick.

Target Variables

A. Supporting leg is bent and heel is pivoted in the direction of the kick. Power is created by proper technique with a positive mental attitude. MOTION WITH EMOTION IS USELESS! Target is the compressor (the breathing system).

B. Rear hand is in guarding position in preparation for countering attack devices. Pull your attacker into the thrust power. Target is knee and/or lower thigh muscle.

C. Use kicks to the lower areas; they are difficult to block and evade. Proper hip rotation into the direction of the thrust increases the total impact. Low kicks open your opponent's defense to face, neck, and chest follow-ups. Targets are groin, hip, and/or attacker's rear leg. Combinations work best.

Countering the Side Kick

A. Remain calm and ready to start your forward motion. Keep hands up for maximum protection against counterattacks. Maintain total eye contact for proper evaluation of attacker.

B. The block and chamber for kicking device are done simultaneously. Rotate the hip completely forward while bringing the leg to the kicking position.

C. In this situation, the elbow up and the reverse palm block are combined to increase effectiveness. Deliver a low round kick to the groin or supporting leg. Use double block to double grab for control.

Countering the Face Front Punch

A. Constant practice is necessary to maintain a good level of technical application. Karate technology best utilizes total mental and physical abilities. The brain, the lungs, and the legs are the best targets when attacking.

B. The essence of Chinese Goju is constant forward motion (CFM) synchronized with the proper technique. A reverse chop changed into a grab neutralizes the face punch and totally exposes the low area to attack.

The Side Kick in Motion

A. Always set your opponent up! Look directly forward into his eyes. Don't ever look at your target. In the Chinese Goju System we try always to use both hands and legs in offensive and defensive maneuvers. Some gung fu styles call this kick the "tiger tail." Relax and concentrate on your target.

B. Start that constant forward motion with the right leg by stepping in the direction of your attacker. At the same time, your left leg goes directly to chamber in preparation for the side kick. Also, this chamber protects the groin and the suspension system. Make sure that you close the distance as swiftly as possible. Keep going!

C. As your knee rises to the chamber position, reach forward with the left hand and grab your attacker's right hand. This grab is a trapping-hand maneuver—it does not allow the attacker the use of the hand for defensive or offensive mechanisms. Always keep your hands in the guard position. This can never be stressed too much. Keep those hands up!

D. Extend your side kick and pull with your left hand. Always pull your attacker in the direction of the total impact force, and always use a tiger claw for the grab. Concentrate on the grabbing and chambering drills in training sessions. It is best to practice this technique with a partner; first on your right side, then on your left. Always start out in slow motion, then fluid motion. Never practice with a partner at full speed; one misdirected technique can injure a person for life. The first rule of training is to be careful. This offensive side kick should be practiced at every training session with at least 20 repetitions on each side. Don't forget to work both sides.

THE ROUND KICK

1. Never kick without an exposed target; and always point your knee in the direction of the target. Use proper footwork to set your opponent up. Never take your eyes off your opponent!

2. Proper chamber protects the lower region while executing kicking techniques. Always move forward with leg attacks to generate more hit power. NOTE: Hand closest to attacker initiates a grab to arm.

3. Pull your attacker into the full rotation of the hip and leg extension. NOTE: Supporting leg is bent and supporting heel has rotated 180° forward. Always hit your target with the instep.

Application in Sparring

A. The round kick is ideal against frontal attacks. Low-kicking techniques are devastating in street situations because the groin and leg are rarely protected.

B. As you start the forward motion, the chamber guards the low regions. The grab is a standard maneuver in the Chinese Goju System. Pull your opponent into the direction of the force.

C. The instep or shin is appropriate when executing the round kick. Try to keep your body erect when executing kicking techniques. At this point, an elbow strike to the back of the head would be the logical follow-up technique.

THE HOOK KICK

1. Setting up the target. Keep rear hand high as guard.

2. Moving forward with cocking action step. Keep legs bent when kicking.

3. Proper chamber. Both hands in defensive posture. Supporting leg is shock absorber.

4A. Snap the hip, knee, and leg forward. At this point, whip your leg back to strike.

4B. (Reverse Angle.) Pulling your leg back in a snapping motion.

5. Keep hands in guard posture throughout kick. Fast hip action.

6. Coming back to chamber after kick develops combination techniques.

NOTE: The hook kick is sometimes referred to as the reverse heel kick. This technique can be executed with the heel or the bottom of the foot. The hook kick and round kick work well in combination. Stress speed and snap.

Practical Application

A. Relax and let your body flow with the technique. NOTE: Front hand is low, rear hand is high—Chinese Goju standard!

B. The hook kick is most commonly applied in combination with techniques like the jab and iron palm. NOTE: Rear cocking step.

C. Proper chamber for maximum effect. Supporting leg is the shock absorber and must be bent throughout all kicking methods.

D. Whip your leg out and snap it back! Impact force is generated by proper hip, leg, and foot action. Set your attacker up!

6. Strategy and Tactics (Confrontation Therapy)

Let us first define strategy in martial arts terms. Strategy is the mental plan of action. Tactics are the physical devices that enact the Speed + Timing + Focus = Maximum Effort (S + T + F = ME. The Natural Law of Martial Arts Science). Self-defense is the ability not to get hit. In a survival situation, the first natural instinct is to survive at all costs. There are basic martial arts principles that cover the art of strategy. In order to get the maximum efficiency from each student who undergoes a confrontation, trauma, behavior modification conditioning is necessary. The psycho-physical cycle of self-defense is reconditioned to enact the proper reflex actions. Simply put, with correct and scientific martial arts conditioning, students can allow their bodies to react to each stimulus with a logical, scientific, and efficient self-defense mechanism.

Most styles of the martial arts are quite limited. The practitioners are not permitted to seek knowledge from forms or styles other than the one in which they are currently at work. It is essential that all styles merge and standardize the strikes and techniques of each individual form of martial arts. I have been involved in the martial arts for over twenty years and have formulated various principles of self-defense. Having been a participant and competitor in over a thousand different martial arts events internationally, in a nutshell, I would say: "Use only what works for you; try not to imitate advanced technique." Let's start with the basic laws of martial arts application.

THE VAN CLIEF LAWS OF MARTIAL ARTS SCIENCES

Chinese Goju is my secret, I bear no arms! May God help me if I ever have to use my art.

1. Love is our law.
2. Truth is our worship.
3. Form is our manifestation.
4. Conscience is our guide.
5. Peace is our shelter.
6. Nature is our companion.
7. Order is our attitude.
8. Beauty and perfection is our life!

Chinese Goju is a total martial arts concept, combining the Eastern and Western philosophies. Martial arts ideology evolves with the environment and relates directly to man's phenomenal ability for adaptation. A proper martial arts education prepares the individual student with the basic tools of life, above all, creative imagination and systematic logic. Every style of the martial arts has something valid to offer so far as practical application is concerned. In order to be valid, a martial art must be effective in self-defense situations. Effectiveness is determined by the outcome of such an encounter, the winner versus the loser. If you have survived a life-and-death situation, you are a winner! Self-defense can simply mean not being in the wrong place at the wrong time. This is where the natural laws of cause and effect apply. If you stay out of trouble, you won't have to get out of trouble. Once you get into trouble, it is hard to get out! Martial arts students excel when it comes to staying out of trouble; martial artists know full well the pains of errors in logic.

But remember, martial arts should *only* be used in emergency situations. Always take your studies with the utmost seriousness. Proper practice, using correct behavior conditioning patterns, minimizes the chance of self-injury during a life-and-death situation. Such a situation is sometimes referred to as "reality" by the students of the martial arts. There are no superior styles, there are only techniques that work and techniques that don't work. Martial arts films have depicted martial artists as supermen. Again, there is no superman, but there is supernormal. *Supernormal* defines the martial arts student who has come to terms with his or her relationship to the world we live in.

Unless you actively practice martial arts, it is impossible to benefit from the mental, spiritual, and physical aspects of the art. Listen to your instructor and analyze what you observe. If you see an instructor trying to teach a senior citizen a flying side kick, you must then question how practical the form or style is. Each particular style should fit the individual student; every technique should be engineered for that person. Martial arts is for everyone, for different purposes. Chinese Goju has become my way of life. It has helped strengthen my character and increased my human growth potential. Having total control of your actions and destiny will solidify your growth potential.

THE VAN CLIEF METHOD OF TECHNICAL APPLICATIONS CHART

Reality Land

Simple Definition: ANYTHING THAT WORKS!

1. Regular practice is necessary to maintain skills.
   NO INPUT equals NO OUTPUT. EQUATION I + O = APPLIED SKILLS.

2. Analyze and memorize how all technique looks during applications to ensure proper form. Correct form in execution does not waste energy. Technique should be smooth and sharp in application. Always ask questions of your instructor or teacher. Never cheat on practical application. Every push-up, punch, and kick prepares you for confrontation therapy.

3. That martial arts are 90% mental and 10% physical is the truth! If your bio-computer (brain) is conditioned properly by your instructor, your physical potential is increased. When a student doesn't understand the origin and purposes of martial arts, he can only be misdirected. Martial arts are for increasing one's growth potential and understanding.

Fantasy Land

Practical Definition: ANYTHING THAT DOESN'T WORK!

1. The belief that practice isn't necessary to maintain and acquire new skills. The condition is called T.R. (Terminal Relaxation). Martial arts students call this disease the Plain Old Laziness!

2. Some advanced students no longer practice basic blocking techniques. Blocking is more important than attacking. It doesn't make any difference on the street if you are a Black Belt or White Belt. If you are hit first in a vital area, you will not be able to counter-attack.

3. Some schools don't practice self-defense. We call this the "bad thinking."

ATTACK ZONES

There are three areas that should be considered the attack zones:
1. The Bio-computer (the human brain)
2. The Compressor (the heart, lungs, vital organs)
3. The Suspension System (foot, ankle, shin, knee, thigh, and hip).

Attack plans should include techniques to all three zones. Kicking techniques to Zones 2 and 3 are most favorable; kicking techniques to Zone 1 are neither logical nor practical. It takes a great deal of proficiency to kick to the head area with maximum power—thousands of repetitions are necessary to perfect such techniques to Zone 1. It is my considered opinion that hand techniques work best in most self-defense situations.

Technique should be practical in application and simple in concept in order to get the most benefit from the execution. Stay in reality land! Understand that self-defense and traditional martial arts are two different total concepts. In self-defense there are no rules, whereas in traditional forms there are rules of physical conduct. Real self-defense means total input, without restrictions. A person who is good at sparring in the dojo would not necessarily be effective in the street.

In general, most schools of martial arts do not practice self-defense. Rather, they practice a prearranged drill called "ippon kumite," which teaches the proper execution of techniques and footwork. But ippon kumite is too prearranged in concept and application. The ippon teaches the student how to react to the attacker's first offensive movement. To be effective, a style must react before the attacker makes his first move! Ippon kumite is normally practiced without realistic blocking/countering mechanisms applied.

Ippon techniques are generally used for demonstrations and exhibitions, not self-defense. Creative instructors try to vary the different offensive and defensive applications to develop a flow of technique. But self-defense cannot be prearranged; it must flow with positive energy. In the Chinese Goju System, I teach the student how to react to the confrontation with a continuous flow of techniques to the vital areas (Zones 1-2-3 must be attacked with every forward motion). Hand techniques are naturally faster than leg maneuvers; it is the speed that is the main priority. Although leg techniques are stronger and can be applied at a greater distance from the attacker, they are slow and predictable in application. These techniques should only be used to get close enough to use hand techniques. Leg techniques cannot be applied in a phone both or taxi cab with maximum effectiveness, whereas hand techniques can be applied at close quarters.

Some styles favor leg techniques over hand techniques, but this is unrealistic. The basic laws of human engineering apply here: you can change the fan belt or battery in your car, but you can't change the parts of your body at a repair shop. Simply, our bodies change with increased age. We as martial artists must change our technical approach to self-defense to acclimate to our ever-changing bodies. With age we lose flexibility and speed, which are necessary components for proper technical expression. The rule of keeping the good and discarding the bad applies here. True students of the martial arts try to refine their art and strip it to the bare essentials. As my teacher, Grandmaster Peter Urban, Tenth Degree Red Belt, says: "Teach every student two blocks, two punches, two kicks!" And Bruce Lee once said to me: "Simplicity is the key to true martial arts application."

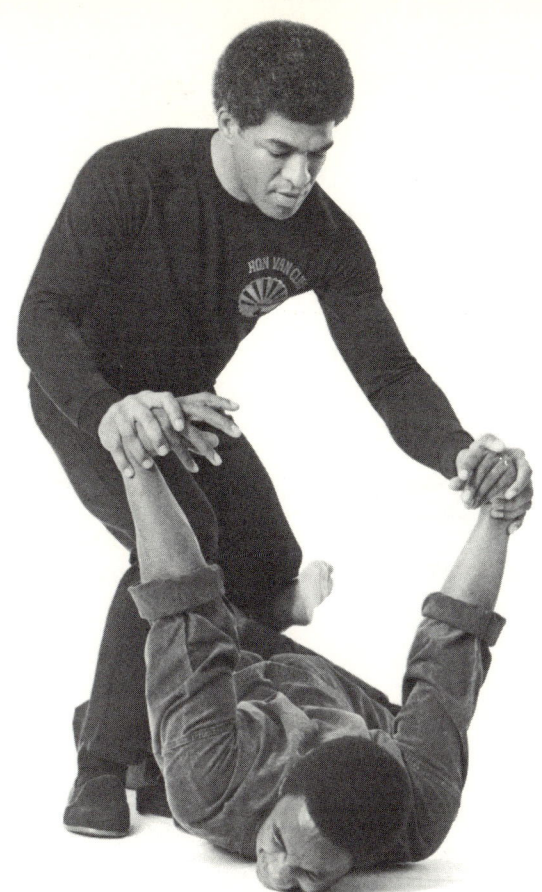

    There are over 165 different styles or forms of martial arts in existence today. Each style has its own particular brand of technical application. The important thing is to choose a form that fits your independent requirements. Before considering the study of martial arts, think first of the amount of time you will need to achieve even minimum proficiency. Then calculate how much time you are willing and able to provide for proper improvement. Do not be impressed by high-ranking instructors who claim supernatural powers and can break boards and bricks. These feats are not applicable to real progress—boards and bricks don't hit back! Such tricks are used to mesmerize the potential student who is looking for commercial exploitation.

    I believe the standardization of the martial arts will put the fantasy-land sifu or sensei out of business. The Better Business Bureau should look into the karate/kung fu school rip-offs. It is ridiculous to think that one person could defeat numerous armed attackers. I have worked in a number of kung fu films and most of the actors don't know anything about the real martial arts; they are experts in martial arts choreography and action direction. Being a fan of the kung fu and samurai films, I was somewhat disappointed and shocked to learn the truth about some of the kung fu superstars. While in Hong Kong on location for *The Black Dragon's Revenge,* I was taken on a tour of the Shaw Brothers and Golden Harvest Film studios, and had occasion to meet some of the superstars of Asia, such as Chen Sing, John Liu, Chan Goon Tai, and Jimmy Wang Yu, to name just a few. Kung fu films are total fantasy land! The big companies in Hong Kong produce assembly-line kung fu films, shooting around the clock. Many of the superstars don't know anything about the martial arts, although they are fine actors. The stuntmen make the stars look good! The action director is the most important man on the shooting set. He is the one who makes dreams into reality. But there is no action director or stuntman in the street, and that's reality land!

TACTICS AND STRATEGY
Multiple Leg Techniques in Combination

1. The first thing to do is size up your opponent. Find his weak points and make a plan before moving in. Your eyes are your radar and viewfinder. Pick your targets by priority.
   1. Bio-computer (head)
   2. Compressor (breathing system)
   3. Suspension System (locomotion mechanism)

   It is ideal to attack all three areas.

2. Close the gap (move in) at full speed and grab with sunfist to the chin or jaw. Always pull in the direction of the strike force for maximum effect. Use the forward momentum to set your opponent up for the follow-up technique, which is, in this situation, a right round kick to the head area.

3. Always use a tight grab to maintain full control of your opponent. Pull him sharply into the full force of your round kick. As you bring the right leg back to the ground, grab with the opposite (left) hand to maintain a balanced flow for the next follow-up technique.

4. Continue the grab and pull action with a side kick to the throat. Keep the right hand up as a safety device against counterattack. And keep the pressure on all the way through the combination. Combination—a continuous series of individual techniques executed at full speed with full power!

5. Apply a wrist lever while chambering for the next technique. A lever is the application of constant pressure to the bones, joints, and/or sockets. Never let your opponent get away from your grasp!
Hold the wrist tightly while executing a low side kick to the knee joint or thigh muscle. Keep your attacker off balance with a constant pulling action coordinated with your attacking mechanisms.

6. Continue the attack plan by delivering a side kick to the ribcage. Never stop your attacking devices until your opponent is down and helpless. There is no such thing as too much technique!
    Remember Van Clief's Law of Survival:
    1. Let's go!
    2. Keep going!
    3. There is nothing else!

The strategy for combat must be flexible if it is to work. Prearranged forms and drills develop one's technical ability, while actual combat (sparring) builds correct timing and the proper mental attitude. Learning how to function under pressure keeps your mind and body honed to a sharp edge. The stress factor is important in conditioning survival mechanisms. Defense is more important than offense! Remember, if you get hit first, the best offensive technique in the world can't help you. Blocking and countering at the same time minimizes the risk factor. Grabbing techniques combined with good footwork allow full control of your attacker. Above all, *think!*

Multiple Arm and Leg Techniques in Combination

1. Pick your target before you move in. Look your man in the eye so as not to telegraph your intentions. Relax, and wait for the right time to strike. Attack with a positive attitude!

2. Close the gap. Grab and kick the groin with a low round kick. The grab and kick are executed at the same time. Prepare for the double kick, low and high. Always use a firm grab and pull your opponent off balance.

3. The groin kick is used as a set-up for the round kick to the face, in one complete movement. If you kick the low region, it will naturally bring the head down. As you bring the kick down, grab with the opposite hand to prepare for the follow-up.

4. As your right leg touches the floor, your left leg goes to chamber for the next kick. Hold the wrist firmly for maximum control. Keep the forward pressure constant (fluid motion). Keep going!

5. Pull your opponent's arm to the outside of your body to give the side kick to the face more extension for power. Notice the right hand remains in the guard position. Always keep your eyes on your opponent! The side kick to the face is the first part of the double kick.

6. Continue your constant forward motion (CFM) with a side kick to the ribcage or the hip joint. The side kick to the face goes directly into the middle side kick without bringing the leg down to the floor. Remember to be flexible!

7. As the left leg retracts and is placed on the floor, shift your right leg forward and deliver a horizontal elbow strike to the chin or jaw. Notice the raised right heel; it generates power and makes the forward movement fluid. Remember to pull the opponent's arm down to assist the impact force with elbow strike.

8. Make sure that his right arm is straight before going to the next technique. Bring the arm to a perpendicular position so that it rests against your left armpit. Your left forearm is the hold, and the right hand keeps his elbow locked. This device is called an arm lever. Make sure it is like a vise. The higher his arm, the lower his body. Keep the pressure tight.

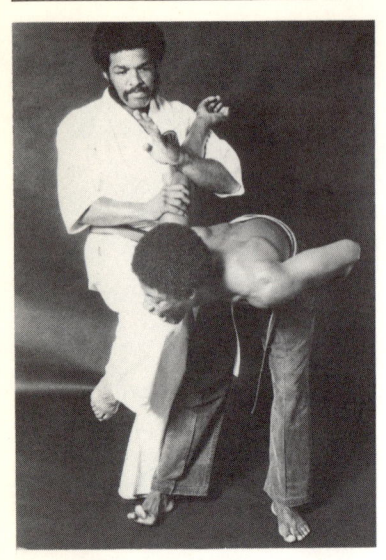

9. Notice how his right arm is locked and held against the body. Remember to keep his arm held high to lower his upper body. At this time, bring up your right knee in a quick, sharp motion to his face. Keep the lever tight!

10. Keep the pressure on. The same hand (left) that held his arm in the hold moves directly to his eyes. Your right hand, which kept his elbow joint locked, executes a downward right elbow strike to the chest or solar plexus. Stay close enough to be always in full control.

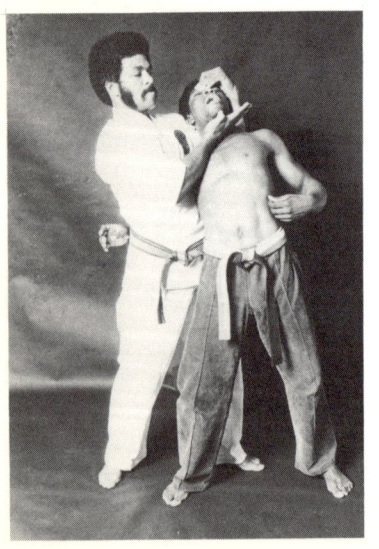

11. Remember, you are in full control of the situation—at this point, he should be helpless. Keep the pressure on his eyes with your fingers. Chop him across the throat with the edge of your hand.

12. Your next move is the double tiger claw. The left hand tears the eyes, the right hand rips the throat. Always stay in motion on the attack.

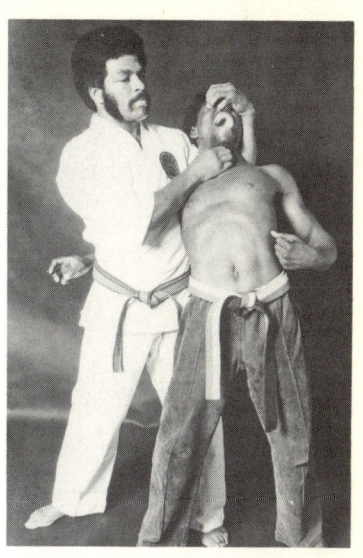

13. Finish him off with a side elbow strike to the solar plexus before you let him drop to the floor. Take your time when executing these 13 techniques.

7. Self-Defense for Women (Evaluation and Practical Application)

Women in the martial arts! I don't believe in the double standard; we are all equal on this planet of ours. In the Chinese Goju System we have designed offensive and defensive mechanisms to fit the specifications of the individual student. There have been many good female practitioners in all of the arts. The first who comes to mind is Sensei Rusty Kanogogi, a legend in the world of judo. She was a terror on the mat! Remember, quality never goes out of style. A skilled woman can be much more lethal than the average male. The element of surprise will completely disorientate a would-be mugger or rapist. It takes very little strength to use the white snake to the eyes or the monkey knee to the groin. Therefore, consider the qualifications of the student, not the gender.

True, some karate styles are not suited to women, due to their high energy output. Sparring in 80 percent of the existing styles involves only head and middle-area targets. On a recent trip to Korea I was shocked to find that in most schools of Tae Kwon Do, hand techniques were not used in sparring. The Tae Kwon Do students were not allowed to grab or sweep. This type of training simply limits the potential for the student's growth.

During my travels in the early 1960s in Asia, I observed many women who had acquired unusual martial skills. But my first real experience of the martial arts came to me in Okinawa (one of the Ryuku Islands, which now belongs to Japan). In those days the Okinawans didn't like the Japanese very much. I was a member of the U.S. Marine Corps stationed at Camp Sukiran, and some fellow Marines were taking karate in a village called Jagaru not far from the base. The sensei was Sumiko Ozawa, about 5 feet 3 inches of Oriental woman. She taught Okinawa-te (Kempo), which was a combination of kung fu and various Okinawan fighting styles. Sensei Ozawa was excellent with weapons. She was outstanding with the sai and bo staff, which are traditional Okinawan weapons, and would spar frequently with all belt levels. Her appearance could easily deceive you into thinking that she had no hit power.

Sensei Ozawa taught me a great deal about the true martial arts spirit. Martial arts education means freedom! I do not recommend sparring for women, since they are not structurally designed to take punches and kicks. But let's just mention some of the famous women in the martial arts: Marion Bermudez (former World Champion), Cynthia Rothrock (international competitor and demonstrator), Angela Mao Ying (kung fu superstar and actress), and Milagros Tirado (international competitor and demonstrator). Ms. Tirado is a three-time All American Champion. Leona Shauble was one of the first American women in sparring competition in the early 1960s. She was a pleasure to watch, beautifully trained in both the mental and the spiritual aspects of the martial arts. Lorna Peterson and Cookie Melendez were quite good at sparring in amateur competition; Cookie Melendez is now involved in full contact sparring and is nationally rated.

It is not important to compete actively. The sport of martial arts is ideal for women as a program of physical and mental fitness plus a form of self-defense. Women students should concentrate on lethal strikes to weak areas. It is best to feign innocence until the proper time to strike. But there are many qualified teachers of the martial arts who just happen to be female. The inclusion of women in the martial arts has been an inspiration to me, and I am currently developing a women's self-defense demonstration team to perform internationally. This is what I call genuine women's liberation.

DEFENSE AGAINST THE STRAIGHT FRONT PUNCH

(Chinese Goju System)

1. This is the standard drilling mechanism called the ippon. Ippons teach correct technical execution, range, focus, and accuracy. Chinese Goju students learn 100 ippons to become a Black Belt. Ippons teach you how to react to your attacker's first move toward you. The proper block combined with the correct counter increases your self-defense ability. Be creative and try anything—you will soon learn whether it works or not. Ippons develop a natural flow of techniques, but techniques must be practiced to be maintained in top form. Creative imagination and systematic logic are the key components of the Chinese Goju ippon. Remember, ippons can be done by anyone, because you have the final choice of technique. Ippons condition you to react properly at the correct time.

2. Make eye contact. Start the bio-computer. Analyze all variables. These are some of the valuable points to remember: *Critical distance, armed/unarmed, height, weight, build.* Relax and breathe normally. LET'S GO!

Your eyes can calibrate the speed and the trajectory of the technique. Be aware and prepare yourself psychologically. Remember the martial arts laws of cause and effect and imagine the structural damage involved. Your bio-computer will activate all self-defense mechanisms if you are properly trained. Reach forward with the right hooking block to immobilize the attacker's right arm. Your left hand goes directly to the guard position automatically. Keep going!

3. Start the constant forward motion (CFM). Reach forward with a hooking block. At the same time, bring your left hand to the guard position. Make sure that you reach far enough out to deflect the punch before it reaches you. Pull down on the hooking block and deliver a front kick to the stomach or groin. Maintain a tight hold on your attacker's forearm and/or wrist. Note the slight bend in the supporting leg to help maintain balance. Remember, middle hooking block and low kick for the counterattack.

4. The right leg delivers a side kick to the ribcage. Pull the person into the force of the kick. Always keep the hand that is not working in the guard position.

5. Continue your natural flow of technique with a side kick to the suspension system. Maintain the constant forward pressure, keeping one hand in the guard position at all times. Remember to bend your supporting leg slightly for balance. The attacks have been low, medium, and low! Always remember that low kicks are very effective in self-defense. Keep going!

6. Continue the combination with a right round kick to the bio-computer. Keep pulling the attacker into the line of force of your kick or punch. This ippon has 1 block and 4 kicks. Most ippons have 5 to 10 techniques, including the blocking mechanism. White Belts should know 5 ippons, Green Belts 20 ippons, Purple Belts 30 ippons, Brown Belts 50 ippons, and Black Belts 100 ippons. Practice your ippons slowly and deliberately. Always concentrate totally when practicing your martial skills.

DEFENSE AGAINST THE REAR GRAB

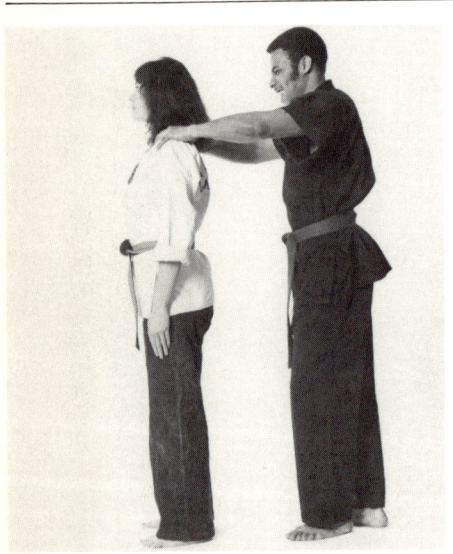

1. Ippons are the primary psycho-physical mechanisms used in the Chinese Goju System of martial arts. Relax and breathe normally. Be aware! An attack from the rear is very hard to defend against. Most women are attacked from the rear in a similar manner. Remember, ippons are psycho-physical drills that help you sharpen your martial skills. Always be creative; do the unexpected. Clear your mind to be as receptive as possible.

It is impossible to foresee an attack from the rear. We must depend on our sensations to prepare our minds and bodies for any emergency. Start your bio-computer!

2. As soon as you feel or sense the touch, react. Use the back kick to the groin area. It is very effective when applied to the low area. Remember, in the street you will have your shoes on! Gung fu practitioners call the back kick the "tiger tail" kick. Always bring one or both hands to the guard position when executing any hand or leg techniques.

3. As you bring your left arm down, shift in the direction of your attacker. Remember the constant forward motion principle! Immediately deliver a left monkey elbow to your attacker's face, using your right hand to assist the left elbow strike. Always close the gap with the legs in order to finish off your attacker. The low kick and the high hand technique should put you in control of the encounter. If not, maintain constant pressure until you are in control. Keep going!

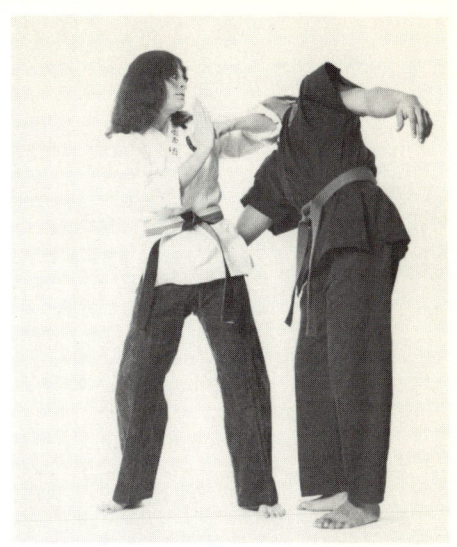

4. The next technique is the aiki-choke. Your left forearm is across the front of the throat; the right forearm is behind the neck. Both hands are clasped tightly to create a condition of high-intensity pain and rapid suffocation. The aiki-choke is a very lethal hold! Always be extremely careful when practicing any self-defense mechanisms. Try to touch both your forearms together for the right effect. Aiki jitsu is one of the arts of the Ninja—the invisible assassins.

This ippon has three offensive techniques. Always try to maintain a constant technique flow and be creative. The psycho-physical drills described in this manual are only drills to stimulate your own imagination. Use anything that keeps you from sustaining structural injury. Ippons should be practiced at every training session.

DEFENSE AGAINST THE FRONT CHOKE

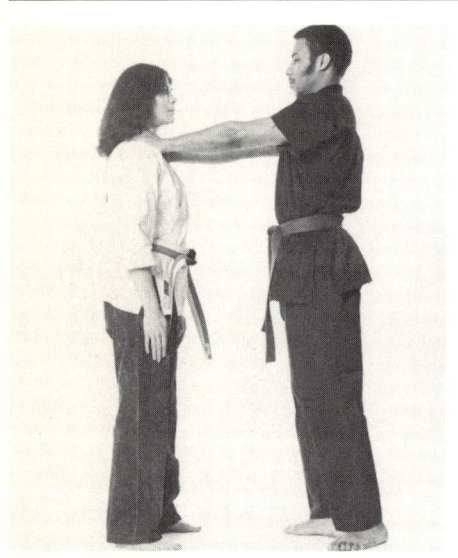

1. Front chokes and rear grabs are the most common attacks against women. If possible, always react before you are actually touched physically. Let's go! Remember, in the real world, *actions have consequences.*

2. Immediately break the choke with a front kick to the groin combined with a double wrist attack. The arms and the legs should work in harmony. Remember to chamber all kicks to get the most output. The front kick can be with the ball or heel of the foot. In the street you can kick with the point of your shoes. Keep going!

3. Your right hand executes a tiger claw grab to the wrist or forearm area. At the same time deliver an iron palm with the left hand to the biocomputer. Remember always to pull in the direction of force.

4. The next technique is an aiki-choke with the left arm. Pressure is applied against the back of the neck with the left forearm. Keep a tight hold by grabbing your wrist. The lack of oxygen combined with the high-intensity pain will cause unconsciousness almost immediately. Always remember to control your techniques when practicing. Anyone can acquire self-defense skills; it just takes patience and practice.

DEFENSE AGAINST THE SIDE GRAB

1. When you practice ippons, always maintain total control over your attacker. The practice of ippons conditions our minds and bodies to work together. It is not sheer power but a combination of flexibility and speed in technical execution that determines the outcome of any confrontation. The side grab is a common attack mechanism. Always be prepared!

2. Immediately start the constant forward action with a monkey elbow to the ribcage. Your left-leg-forward step increases the hit power of the monkey elbow. Remember, your first offensive technique should put you in control of your attacker. The opening created by the monkey elbow allows you to follow up with a series of devastating techniques. Keep going!

3. Your left hand delivers a back fist strike to the temple area. Always keep one hand in the guard position for security and never lose sight of your attacker. Maintain a constant flow of effective techniques to eliminate the possibility of counterattack. Take total control of the situation—never give your attacker a moment to breathe!

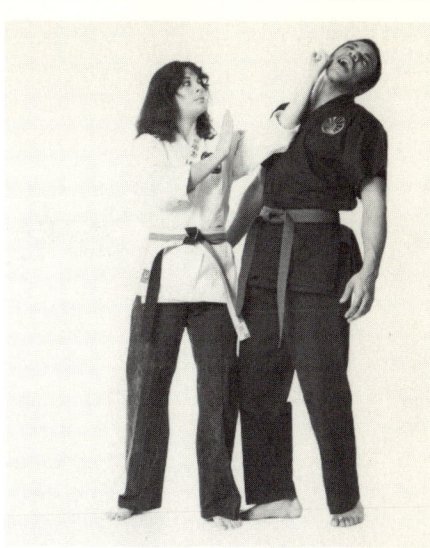

4. Immediately execute the double tiger claw to the neck or shoulder area. Observe how the attacker is on the balls of his feet. This means total control—at this point your attacker is at your mercy. It is always better to use too much technique than not enough. Concentrate all your power into the double tiger claw technique. In Chinese Goju, we call this the set-up.

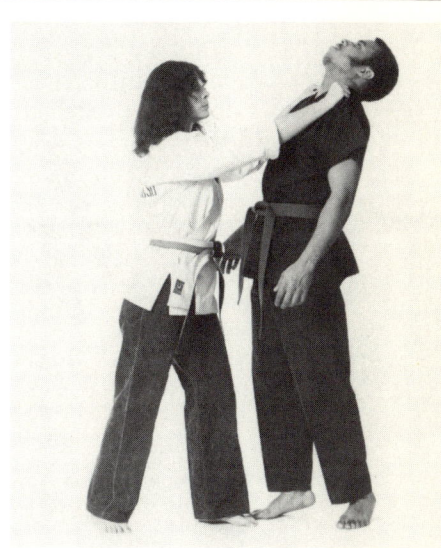

5. Pull your attacker downward into the rising monkey knee. Striking the groin and breathing system should have the same effect. This technique, if practiced properly, should knock your attacker out. This ippon contains four techniques that not only do structural damage but create high-intensity pain. The equation for unconsciousness is high-intensity pain combined with devastating structural attacks. Practice your self-defense at every training session. One half of every Chinese Goju program is self-defense training. Be creative and develop your own combinations of technique. Creative imagination and systematic logic determine the outcome of confrontation therapy. Train hard and always THINK!

DEFENSE AGAINST THE FRONT LUNGE KNIFE ATTACK

1. Always stay out of range until you can create an opening or the attacker commits himself. The only real way to handle a knife attack is to close the gap to render the attacker's knife useless. The only advantage of any weapon is distance. When a person uses a weapon, he tends to concentrate only on the weapon's potential. He never uses the rest of his body to maximum effect. Your eyes are the radar and rangefinder for attacking devices.

2. As the attacker lunges toward you, start your constant forward motion. The appropriate personal action would be to sidestep the frontal attack. Use the body pivot or the sidestep principle to avoid attack. Use your bio-computer. Let's go!

3. The second movement of the Black Dragon Blocking System would be the logical technique. The right hand deflects the right forearm of the attacker's arm. After deflection, always grab for total control. The tiger claw to the forearm is best for this situation. The left hand simultaneously executes the iron palm to the ribcage, which is totally unprotected at this time. Always pull your attacker into the line of the main impact force. Keep going—you are in total control of the situation. From here on, maintain a constant flow of technique.

4. The left sunfist to the chin or neck would be the most logical variable in this situation. Grab and punch at the same time. Set yourself up for the next technique.

5. The left leg delivers a round kick to the temple area. Always pull in the direction of the main strike force. This kick, if properly applied, totally disorientates your attacker psychologically and structurally affects the bio-computer and neck. It is best to use a double tiger claw with the round kick. Keep going!

6. Follow up with a left round kick to the groin. Computer shock with structural damage puts the attacker out. The impact of a properly applied groin kick is tremendous.

7. Continue your constant forward motion with a left tiger claw and right iron palm to the chin. The tiger claw controls the left arm and directly increases the hit power with the pulling action. Push and pull mechanisms—there are over 1,000 techniques in the Chinese Goju System. You have unlimited variables at your disposal. Remember, "Practice makes perfect."

DEFENSE AGAINST THE OVERHEAD KNIFE ATTACK

1. Be aware! Your eyes start your psycho-physical self-defense mechanisms. Close the gap to limit the knife variables. Relax and concentrate totally. Let's go!

2. The right leg moves forward as the right hand executes the rising block. Your left hand delivers a sunfist to the ribcage. Remember to combine force with forward motion for maximum effectiveness.

3. The next technique is the double tiger claw. Your right hand controls his right forearm and wrist. At the same time, your left hand claws his right shoulder muscles. The knife should drop to the floor at this time due to muscle spasms. The tiger claw creates high-intensity pain with muscular reaction.

4. Keep going! Use the double tiger claw to pull your attacker into the rising monkey knee to the elbow joint area. If this technique is applied properly, the arm will be broken.

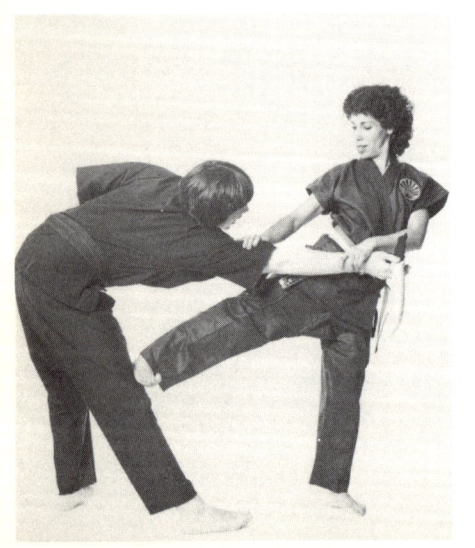

5. Maintain total control. Deliver a side kick to the thigh muscle or knee to disable the suspension system. Ippons are the best form of self-defense practice.

6. Continue the total pressure with the monkey knee to the right elbow joint. Note the double tiger claw techniques to the bicep muscle and the forearm and wrist. Concentrate all your power into your fingers to make the claws have the most effect. After the total shock phase, the control stage will engage itself automatically.

7. Maintain total control until the knife drops to the floor. Only then should you stop offensive action. Your attacker is still considered dangerous to you. Remember this is just a drill to cultivate your creative imagination through technical expression.

8. The final technique is an aiki-choke—sometimes called the coiling snake. This technique cuts off the oxygen source immediately. Remember the equation: shock + pain = knockout! Good self-defense takes a lot of hard work.

SELF-DEFENSE

1. Ready Posture—Relax! Breathe in through the nose and exhale through the mouth. Shoulder-width stance so that weight is naturally balanced; legs should be bent slightly at the knees.

2. Overhead Strike: Keep your eyes on your attacker. Sidestep while moving forward (Black Dragon Blocking System). "Always try to block and hit at the same time."

3. As the attacker's arm descends, you move forward on an angle to your opponent's exposed side. At this time, you execute a high block with mid-section punch. NOTE: This technique is the first in the Black Dragon Blocking System. Keep shoulders straight when punching, in the front stance.

4. Follow up the grab for finishing technique, e.g., knee strikes and elbow strikes. NOTE: Always pull with grab. Keep forward motion while executing techniques. Leg techniques are used to get close enough for hand techniques.

5. Pull your attacker into the side kick to the throat. The grab and pull generates more impact force when punching and kicking.

THE PHOENIX ATTACKS

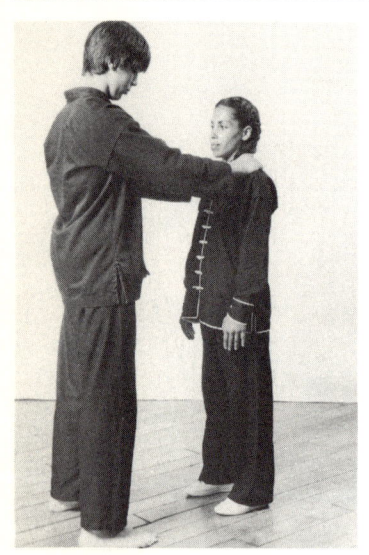

A. Front shoulder grab—Relax. Prepare to attack the wrists with the forearms in a semicircular pattern.

B. Aiki jitsu—Attack the body's weak points. Push down with arms against the wrists to escape.

C. Pull arm or wrist down to attack eyes with Snake style. Keep moving forward with technique explosion.

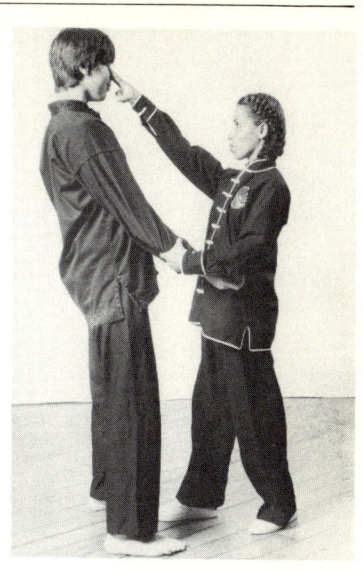

D. Dragon palm to neck or chin target. NOTE: Opposite hand attacks mid-section.

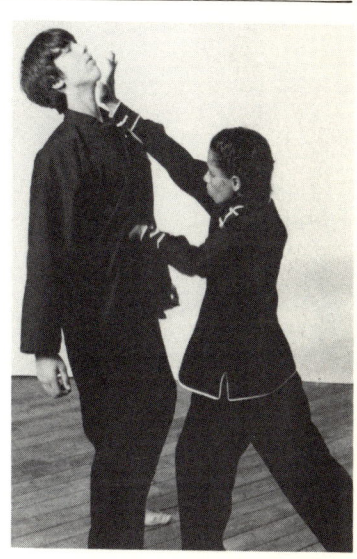

E. Finish with side kick to face or neck. Kicks and punches work best with grab for effect.

F. Single wrist grab—white snake to eyes with counter grab.

G. Pull into groin kick with instep or heel striking surface.

H. Ten dragon palm to neck and breathing system.

NOTE: Remember constant forward motion with combination techniques.

I. Upward elbow strike to jaw. NOTE: Pull down with upward elbow. Keep close to attacker for control and technique variables.

J. Double grab with knee to face attack. NOTE: The knee is very effective to groin, stomach, and face targets.

K. Pull down with downward elbow strike to the neck (base of brain).

L. Ninja choke while pulling attacker backward and off balance. Constant pressure with forearm to throat area.

NOTE: The Phoenix
Quick flurries to vital areas with sharp snapping motions. Constant motion. Make attacks creative, constant, and devastating!

THE PHOENIX ATTACKS: SELF-DEFENSE

Countering the Wrist Grab

A. Single wrist grab—pull down and knee to groin. Supporting leg is bent throughout kicking. Toes are pointed down and relaxed.

B. As knee starts down, elbow initiates face attack. Pull your attacker into the direction of form to generate more impact power.

C. Semicircular elbow strike to temple or jaw targets. Keep your body moving forward with all attack procedures.

D. Moving in with double tiger claw attacks. Left hand claws the eyes and face as the right hand reaches for the groin grab. The tiger starts with the palm and completes with the fingers.

E. The tiger seizes the sheep... Maximum shock with tiger palms initiates the tiger claw technique to completion of techniques. NOTE: Constant forward motion.

F. Pull down grab with elbow strike to neck, temple, or chin. NOTE: The tiger claw works very well with the monkey elbow. Thai boxers have many times proved the effectiveness of the elbow in combat.

NOTE: From A to F, the motion should be constant and with full speed and mental attitude. Motion with emotion has tremendous effect. In martial arts, there are no men and women, just martial artists!

Rule No. 2: Render your attacker helpless, but try not to do structural damage (fractures, contusions). "Use only what is necessary"—RVC.

G. The rear grab—Move to the rear with reverse monkey elbow to breathing system. Sometimes it is possible to step down on your attacker's shin or ankle while setting up the reverse monkey elbow. Note the short stance for mobility.

H. Pull with right hand into tiger palm strike to chin. The hit with the tiger palm is hard, but the pressure is constant to raise the attacker's chin so that it will be impossible for him to see anything. This, of course, is the set-up for the next technique. NOTE: Stay close to attacker to minimize counterattack.

I. Double tiger claw with monkey knee to face. The knee moves up as the hands pull down, for maximum effect. Desirable targets are neck, face, chest, for the monkey knee. NOTE: Supporting leg is in bent position while the elbows are pulled in to protect the face and body.

J. Pull with right hand with monkey elbow to jaw or temple area. NOTE: Keep motion constant! Develop flow with variable technique. Always keep fluid and in command of the situation.

K. Left hand grabs to execute right iron palm to chin. NOTE: Don't stop until the mission is completed. Rule No. 1: Don't get hit first! "Defense is just as important as offense"—RVC.

8. Self-Defense for Senior Citizens (Practical Application)

Martial arts is the perfect cardiovascular exercise—I have personally taught students from three years of age to eighty-one years of age. The Chinese Goju style changes with your body. Karate becomes aiki jitsu, meaning total control. In the true art of aiki jitsu there are no hand or leg strikes; aiki jitsu is the practical application of control devices such as levers, holds, and locks. The longer you practice, the better your abilities become. Remember, physical and mental input creates total expression.

DEFENSE AGAINST THE OVERHEAD HAMMER STRIKE

1. Relax and breathe normally. Depend on your senses to activate your self-defense mechanisms. Whatever you do, commit yourself! Start the bio-computer.

2. The Black Dragon Blocking System is most effective against short-range weapons like knives, sticks, chains, and bats. The element of surprise is a great advantage. Muggers are really surprised when they become the victims of a senior citizen's attack! The left hand blocks the right forearm with the rising block. Never block a weapon with your hand or arm; always block the wrist or forearm to prevent the weapon from injuring your body. Move smoothly from technique to technique. Combinations of technique must flow like electricity.

3. The double tiger claw will control the arm with the weapon. Concentrate all of your power into the fingers. Mentally prepare for the next technique. Breathe normally when executing any technique. The double tiger claw, if applied correctly, will neutralize the hammer. Keep going!

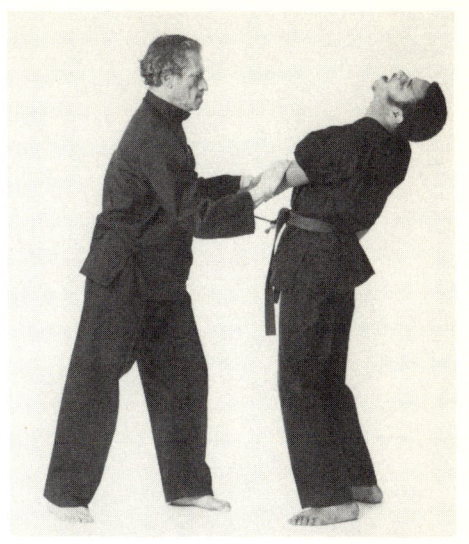

4. Pull your target toward your chambered leg in preparation for a kicking attack. The chamber also guards your lower area from counterattack. Always stay on guard.

5. Continue your pulling action and deliver a side kick to the knee joint. Note the right hand is in the guard position as usual. The kick to the suspension system will eliminate any further counterattack. Use only what is necessary. If applied correctly and to the right target, the side kick can be devastating.

DEFENSE AGAINST THE FRONT GRAB

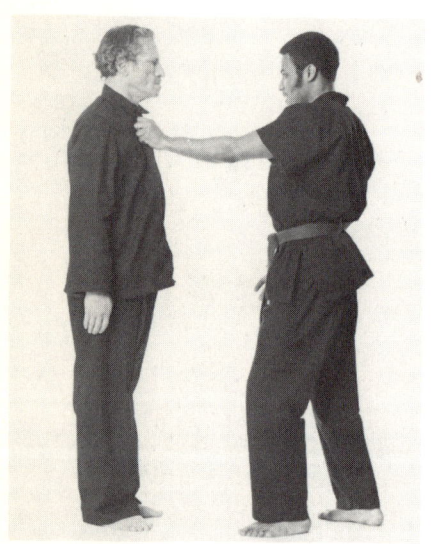

1. Let's go! Concentrate totally on your attacker. Relax and breathe normally; make eye-to-eye contact; don't resist the grab! Any action at this time would cause a reaction that could not be predicted. Therefore start the bio-computer and prepare the life-support mechanisms for action.

2. The left forearm traps your attacker's grabbing arm. Your right hand assists to increase the pulling potential. This technique is called an aiki-lever. It creates high-intensity pain in the joints and limbs involved. If pressure is increased, fracture or dislocation follows. Remember the constant forward motion principle. Keep going!

3. It is my opinion that karate takes too much of a high energy output. Aiki jitsu is a low energy form of self-defense. Speed and control are the key factors of the self-defense mechanisms. Aiki jitsu and karate are both forms of control. Karate controls through shock created by impact force against the body; aiki jitsu controls without hit power. There are no punches or kicks in true aiki jitsu. Control is acquired through various psycho-physical mechanisms such as holds, levers, locks, sweeps, and chokes. All force is deflected rather than met head on.

4. The final technique in this drill is a three-way lever. This comes from the Snake style of gung fu. The left arm coils around the attacker's left elbow. Your right hand holds the wrist with the tiger claw technique in a downward pushing motion. It is this downward action, combined with the control lever on the elbow joint, that produces constant pressure. The shoulder, elbow, and wrist can be broken or dislocated with little effort. Combine the aiki jitsu with the karate to come up with self-defense mechanisms. Maintain a tight grip with the tiger claw and the aiki-lever for maximum effect.

DEFENSE AGAINST THE REAR GRAB

1. This is the time when all that training and sweating pays off! Relax to prepare the body for immediate action. Maintain a normal breathing pattern. Inhale through the nose and exhale through the mouth. Let's go!

2. Bring your right hand to the guard position and start your constant forward motion. Your left hand starts the coil over both forearms in a semicircular arc. If the left hand moves, the left leg must move. Remember, the Snake is a very efficient style of self-defense, emphasizing control over any limb that comes within contact range. Keep going!

3. The left forearm controls both arms with the "coiling snake" technique. The right hand is in the guard position prepared for counterattack or for the delivery of hand techniques. Remember, to be effective, this hold must be tight.

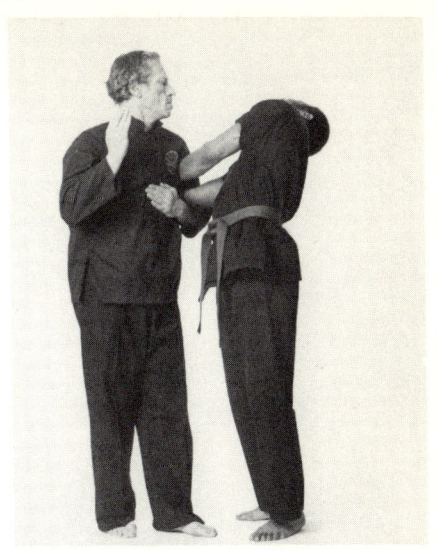

4. Your right iron palm hits the attacker on the chin and continues to push the head back. Remember the palm up, head back rule! You are now in complete control of the situation.

5. The left monkey knee to the groin should be sufficient to incapacitate any would-be mugger. It is at this point that the mugger becomes the victim!

6. The next technique is the double tiger claw to the neck and shoulder muscles. Maintain that constant forward motion of technique. Never lose eye contact. Concentrate on every one of your moves. The "iron will" activates our supernormal capabilities.

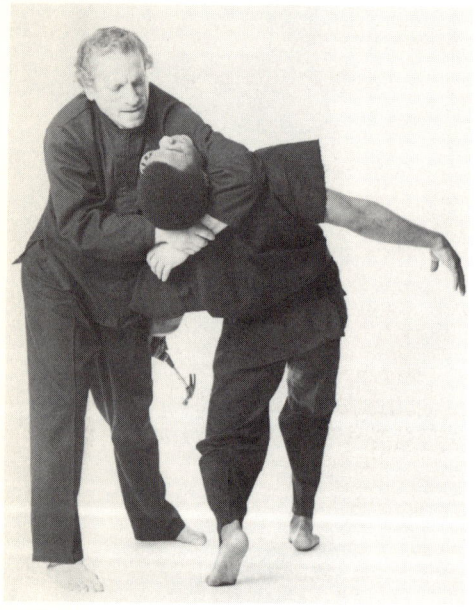

7. The final technique is an aiki jitsu choke. The left arm traps the neck while the right arm assists. This technique is referred to as the reverse head lock in Chinese wrestling (Goti). Goti was a form of ancient Mongolian wrestling. This technique cuts off breathing mechanisms, which knocks the attacker out.

Always remember that aiki jitsu works very well with karate arts. The Ninja were very adept at silent technique. Every Ninja was taught the martial arts, with emphasis placed on weapons, aiki, and karate. Master Ronald Duncan is an American Ninja. He has been a great source of knowledge in Ninja traditions and technology and has traveled worldwide demonstrating his arts. Master Duncan is certainly a credit to the world of martial arts.

9. Martial Arts Education for Children (Form and Application)

Children seem to be the most receptive group of all to martial arts education. They are inexhaustible! Watching children train in the martial arts is a wonderful experience.

I believe that children should not spar until the age of ten, when their bodies are stronger and concentrative abilities have been formed. My son Ron started his martial arts education at the age of two. While in his playpen Ron would do techniques that amazed me. He is five and a half now and trains regularly in the group classes. He has developed discipline and the ability to concentrate on correct technique application. A proper martial arts education can only enhance a child's development.

Of course, children must be made to realize that martial arts is not a game. Never allow playing during a training session, and always supervise all classes. You and your child should read this together!

DEFENSE AGAINST THE WRIST GRAB

1. The wrist grab is a common technique in child abuse or molestation. Be aware—never talk to strangers. If possible, never allow a child to travel without an adult. Don't resist the grab. Let's go!

2. Let out a loud scream if anyone is in the vicinity! Bring your right leg to chamber in preparation for kicking techniques. Keep your eyes on your attacker. Stay calm and breathe normally. In the Navy we sound "battle stations," which means the state of complete alert!

3. Your right leg kicks with the low front kick to the mid-thigh or knee area for maximum effect. Your left hand goes directly to the guard position as usual.

4. Use the double tiger claw to pull your attacker downward in preparation for the next technique in the combination. Keep going—there is nothing else. Use your body weight plus the double tiger claw to bring the arm down.

5. Keep a tight grip on the wrist and forearm. Close the distance with a rising monkey knee into the attacker's forearm. Pull down, knee up. Always bend the supporting leg to ensure centerline balance.

6. The final technique is the side kick to the knee or thigh area. This kick is very painful. At this time the attacker will let go of your wrist. Seize this opportunity to run away from the immediate area to find some help. Escape and evasion is the name of the game. A sound martial arts education will prepare the child for the violent world that we live in. The mental and physical benefits of the martial arts will stay with him or her for the rest of life.

DEFENSE AGAINST THE ATTEMPTED FRONT GRAB

1. Note the difference in height. A child may use this advantage to attack the lower unprotected areas. Relax and breathe normally. Remember the escape and evasion principle! Bio-computer on, your body is in a state of total alert.

2. Sometimes you may be able to react before there is physical contact. But if you cannot escape, you must resort to your martial skills. Remember, never resist a grab unless it is to a vital area such as the neck. Always try to react before you are physically touched.

3. Your left side kick should hit the knee. Always lean in on your kicking technique for additional hit power. The right hand goes directly to the guard position. Your left hand is actually a tiger claw technique. Always pull your attacker into the direction of force.

4. The final technique in this drill is the front heel kick to the groin. This kick will allow you to leave the area without physical harm. A fast kick to the groin can cause serious damage even from a child. Remember the element of surprise! Always leave the scene of violence, whether you are involved or not.

DEFENSE AGAINST STRANGERS WITH CANDY

Never accept anything from a stranger! Always remember this principle. It is best just to leave and not even answer the stranger's questions. Be alert to any aggressive vibrations.

1. Unfortunately, there are too many bad people in the world. Teach your children how to stay out of trouble. Remember, stress and tension affect children, too. Martial arts can be the perfect exercise to help relieve that stress.

2. Bring your left leg directly to the chamber position in preparation for offensive leg techniques. Never lose eye contact with your attacker.

3. The final technique is the left side kick to the groin with the heel. Extend your leg fully into the target. This kick will cause the attacker to release his grip on you. If possible, always pull in the direction of the main strike force to amplify the hit power. It is best to teach children self-defense and kata until their teens so as not to jeopardize the child's health. Sparring should never be done with children under 10 years of age—there are too many variables to consider and no one should ever spar without protective equipment. But martial arts build good character and a very positive outlook on life.

10. Advanced Self-Defense
The Chinese Goju System
(Animal Forms in Self-Defense)

The animal forms are very efficient for self-defense. Most animal forms require the use of a partner to apply the various techniques realistically. The martial arts employ training aids to supplement the standard operating procedures. For example, sandbags are necessary in the study of the Tiger style and iron balls are necessary to develop hand coordination and finger strength. Training aids are necessary to the development of the martial arts. Sometimes a wooden man with five arms is used by the students of the Snake style. I am familiar with twelve animal forms of Chinese Gung Fu: the Snake, Tiger, Monkey, Crane, Bear, Dragon, Praying Mantis, Eagle Claw, Leopard, Phoenix, Elephant, and Horse.

During the last twenty-five years of my martial arts education, I have learned that one never ceases to learn! I met a great gung fu master in Taiwan who claimed to know twenty animal styles—too bad I didn't stay in Taiwan long enough to check him out! The confrontation had very interesting possibilities. Another Chinese gung fu master claimed to be able to deliver fifteen punches in three seconds. He challenged me to a full contact match and never showed up. Bruce Lee once told me that he was challenged numerous times in Hong Kong. Challenges are never worth the bother. In the martial arts there is always someone better—get back to reality!

The animal styles of gung fu are quite fascinating and effective as forms of self-defense. It would take at least two volumes to cover the numerous styles in detail, but this chapter gives you a practical look at the basic forms: the Monkey, Tiger, and Snake.

    I was given the name "Hok Lung," which means Black Dragon, by Grandmaster Leung Ting of Wing Tsun Kuen. Sifu Leung Ting has influenced my gung fu education in a most positive way: to watch him practice the 108-movement form on the wooden man is hypnotic (Wing Tsun practitioners use the wooden man in their daily training sessions). Another gung fu master who really impressed me was Sifu Leo Fong of Stockton, California. I was in Manila on location filming *The Bamboo Trap,* with Leo Fong and Darnell Garcia. Leo taught me some of the basics of the Tiger Claw style, being himself a student of arnis, Filipino stick- and knife-fighting arts. He introduced me to Grandmaster Remy Presas, "the father of modern arnis."

    During my four-month stay in the Philippines, I practiced martial arts with Leo and Remy almost every day at my hotel. One day Leo and I were sparring in the hotel. I learned that Leo had a terrific left hook and powerful kicking techniques. Most gung fu practitioners don't use kicking techniques or left hooks, but Leo had been a professional boxer in his youth. I will always be grateful to Leo and Remy for the wisdom they imparted to me. Leo Fong made me realize how necessary training aids like heavy bags, speed bags, and bean bags can be. Remy Presas taught me the basic rudiments of arnis. His speed with the rattans (an extension of the empty hand) was blinding! Leo and Remy inspired me so much that I began documenting my martial arts experiences. Leo also studied Wing Tsun with Bruce Lee. Leo and I practiced "sticky hands," sensitivity hand drills, on many occasions. Now I am happy to share these experiences with you. Remember, martial arts knowledge must be shared with the world.

Animal Forms in Self-Defense

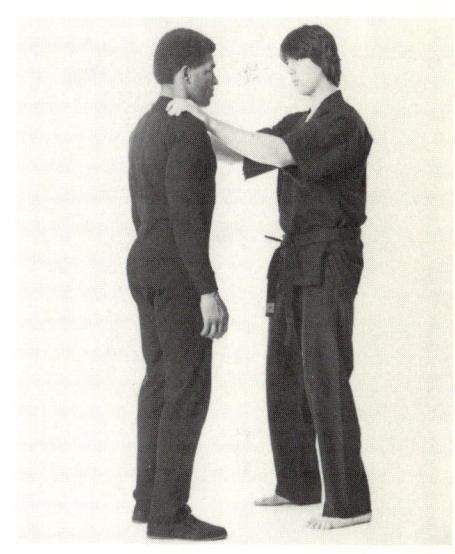

1. Relax and breathe normally. Start your bio-computer and activate all life-support mechanisms. Don't resist the force of the front grab. Never lose eye contact with your attacker! Immediately activate self-defense mechanisms. Commit yourself totally in personal, positive action. Motion + Emotion = Maximum Effort.

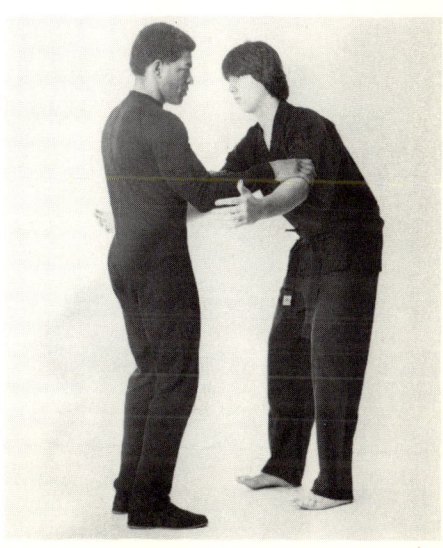

2. Reach up through the attacker's arms, execute a double tiger claw to the upper arm, and rip the muscles. Remember, first the palm then the fingers strike and rip the bicep. Concentrate on the downward slapping and tearing motions. Always put your full body into both offensive and defensive maneuvers. Gung fu masters of old could tear bark from trees with the tiger claw.

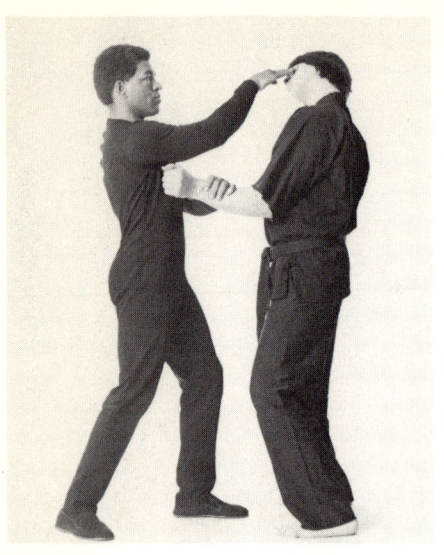

3. Immediately cross-grab the attacker's left hand and execute the white snake strike to the eyes. Always pull your opponent into the strike force. The cross-grab is actually a tiger claw on the forearm.

   Always maintain a constant forward motion. Remember to relax the striking hand until the moment of contact. Coordinate the cross-grab with the eye attack for maximum economy of motion. You are controlling and attacking at the same time.

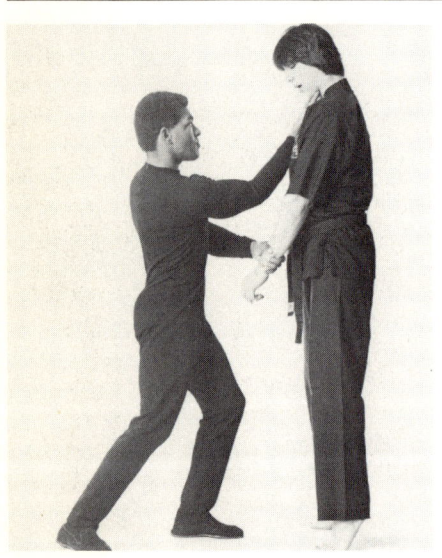

4. Move directly from the eye stab to a tiger claw to the throat with the right hand. The left hand maintains a constant pulling action downward. The result of the tiger claw is the immediate shutdown of the breathing system (the compressor). Remember the constant forward motion principle.

5. Finish your attack plan with the monkey knee to the groin area. Make sure that you pull your attacker down into the rising knee action. Use the double tiger claw technique to maintain total control. The tiger, snake, and monkey techniques work very well together. Study of the animal forms will add to your arsenal for self-defense.

Practical Application

A. Sometimes you may be confronted with more than one attacker. This ippon will prepare you for just that. You must take action immediately. Let's go!

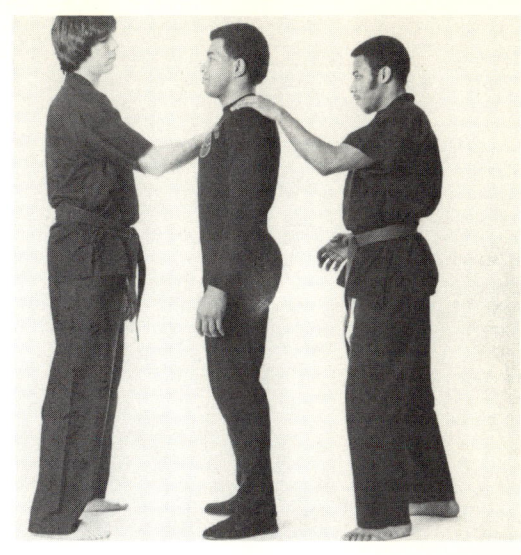

B. Instantly execute the double tiger claw technique. Your right hand attacks the throat while your left hand attacks the groin. Always use your palms in a slapping motion. The grab and ripping motion must be as tight as possible for effectiveness. Speed and accuracy are the two major factors in self-defense.

C. The next technique comes from the Snake style. This is the escape and control device. Your arms reach up and over your attacker's forearms to create an aiki jitsu lever on the elbow and shoulder. The coiling of the snake is the action of your forearms circling the attacker's arms. Bend forward slightly to increase the effectiveness of this particular trapping hand mechanism.

D. Follow up with a technique from the Monkey style for total control. "The monkey grabs the melons" is the classical terminology used in various monkey forms. Let your snake technique flow directly into the Monkey style. The last two techniques create high-intensity pain, and bone, muscle, and joint injuries. Let your energy flow, and keep going!

E. "The monkey grabs the melons" is actually an aiki-choke and lever mechanism. Make a complete circle with both arms that terminates with both palms placed on the chest or as high as possible. Always keep your forearms as tight around the neck as possible for maximum effect. Aiki jitsu techniques work well with the various other martial arts. Self-defense mechanisms should be as simple as possible to comprehend and execute; flashy techniques don't work in the street. Only the practical, tactical ones work.

IRON BROOM AND DRAGON TAIL SWEEPS COMBINATION

1. The monkey sweep is a favorite among Chinese Goju practitioners because of its deceptiveness. It is commonly used as a counterattack mechanism against high-kicking assaults or the front lunge hand attacks to the head area. Never look at where you are going to attack (telegraphing). Let your eyes see and focus on the whole body, not one specific area. Always be aware!

2. As you drop down and pivot forward, keep your eyes on the target. Never put your knee on the ground; rotate on the ball of your foot. Your hands will stabilize your spin. Pivot on your left foot and deliver the low round kick with the right leg to the leg closest to you. Prepare to retract the kicking leg and place it in front of you for the next technique.

3. Bring the right leg back to you to a comfortable position. Start the forward hip motion as soon as it is placed on the ground. Never take your eyes off the target. Keep in mind that you should be fluid and continuous in motion. Any hesitation could prove fatal.

4. Spin on the ball of the right foot to complete the circle. Remember the constant forward motion (CFM) principle! As you turn on the right foot, start the cocking action of the left leg for the dragon tail sweep. Do not lock the knee when using the dragon tail; it will cause injury to the knee joint. Never spin on your knee.

5. The dragon tail is a Chinese Goju standard. It can be used against both legs to drop the attacker to the ground. The low spinning round kick is the "iron broom," which is less versatile than the dragon tail. The combination of the two techniques is known as the "Monkey sweep." The dragon tail has the same effect as being hit with a baseball bat across the legs; either the front or back of the legs will do the job!

6. The monkey sweep is the most effective suspension attack mechanism. When applied properly, the monkey sweep is capable of breaking the leg of an adult male. Besides impact power, the knees and ankles receive tremendous unbalanced pressure. If you destroy your attacker's legs, you immediately achieve superiority! Seize any opportunity.

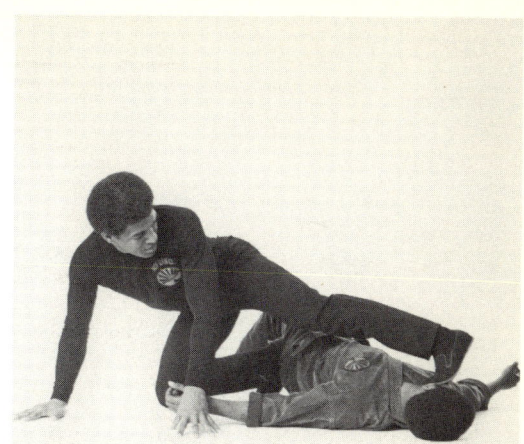

11. The Alphabet of Martial Arts (Chinese Goju Technology)

Awareness—The finding of one's self. To become in tune with the universe, you must first know who you are, why you are, and where you are in relationship to the rest of the cosmos. The first principle of the Chinese Goju System is: Defeat the self, first to know! When you understand yourself, you understand humanity. Always stay in a condition of mental and physical awareness. Know your potential and limitations to formulate a good framework of reality. Remember, awareness is reality.

Behavior—Behavior is a reflex action. Learning is a change in performance as a result of correct repetition. Practice is reinforced repetition of psycho-physical drills to increase total efficiency. The aim of Chinese Goju conditioning is to increase individual growth potential and total emotional expression. Behavioral pattern conditioning is the motivation necessary to stimulate increased results. Develop and maintain good physical fitness habits for life.

Conditioning—This means the actual physical and mental outputs in performance of martial skills. Chinese Goju kata (sets, forms) are designed to keep the cardiovascular system in top shape by making the body work hard and demanding increased amounts of oxygen over an extended period of time. Proper training combined with a healthy mental attitude increases total potential. But fitness is a temporary achievement. The condition of fitness must be maintained through regular, consistent psycho-physical mechanisms. In the real world of martial arts, we refer to these mechanisms as *work*. Never lose your fitness level; believe in total lifelong fitness.

Design—For any martial art to be effective, human engineering must be taken into consideration. The Chinese Goju System is unique in its design, being tailored to meet the necessary requirements of each student. An understanding of the science of human engineering is the foundation of a proper martial arts education. Techniques must pass the tests of time and efficiency to be considered practical. The bottom line is, does a particular technique work or not? Techniques should be easy to understand and simple to execute. Simplicity is the key word—be practical and economical.

Energy—There are two types of energy in the martial arts: mental energy and physical energy. We don't create or destroy energy, our bodies are energy-converters. Anything we consume is either burned up as exercise energy or stored in the body as fat. So, we must not waste energy! Be practical and economical when executing technique. The combination of the "iron will" (see below) and good structural design gives the student total energy output. The Mind + The Body = Harmony. Chi Gung, or physical energy, means the ability to change energy into "hit power." Hit power is the amount of concentrated-force energy measured in pounds per square inch. Simply, the effect of your offensive techniques. Could you knock out an attacker in a street situation? Remember, the mental, physical, and spiritual balance you achieve will be directly proportionate to the amount of applied-force energy.

Fluidity—Fluidity is the technical language of martial arts. The ability to execute effective hand and leg techniques takes many years of practice. To attain fluidity, you must maintain a constant forward motion (CFM) when delivering offensive and defensive techniques. Keep going! Technique is your ammunition, your body the weapon. Be versatile and creative in your technique. Constant forward motion creates momentum, which adds to the hit-power potential. Always remember that change is constant.

Growth—The value of a martial arts education is the ability to function in an orderly manner in a disorderly society. Growth can be measured by one's ability to use skills attained through the martial arts in everyday life. Growth is the understanding that nothing is impossible. Some people think that having technical abilities is growth; this is erroneous. Growth has nothing to do with martial skills. The martial arts experience is psychological growth.

Health—We as living machines are responsible for our own maintenance for the duration of our lives. Martial arts are the perfect exercise for our bodies! Mental health means having a proper framework of reality. Physical health means the reality of a total lifelong fitness program. Fitness is a temporary condition that requires continual maintenance. The optimum exercise pattern should be every other day, to give the body enough time to recuperate. And remember, you are what you eat. Never eat junk food. A proper diet combined with a sensible exercise program will put you on the road to total fitness.

There are five other types of fitness programs used in martial arts: *aerobic, anaerobic, isometric, isotonic* and *isokinetic*. Aerobic exercise must have a steady, rhythmic type of action that consumes large amounts of oxygen; jogging and rope jumping are fine examples of aerobics. Anaerobic exercise is physical action that takes place very rapidly or explosively, as in sparring. Isometric exercise concentrates on building strength and muscle tone. Isometrics create resistance without movement; they are somewhat limited, because they don't develop speed and flexibility. Isotonic exercise is my favorite exercise for power conditioning.

Interest—Interest is referred to by Chinese Goju practitioners as "motivational therapy." It is entirely up to the instructor how far the student will develop in the martial arts. The teacher must stimulate the student's interest by setting the right example. Teaching ability must be combined with creative imagination to communicate the martial arts message. We are all students—I learn something new every day by observing the lower-ranking belts. Interest is stimulated by positive progress. Only students who are highly motivated will achieve technical proficiency. No matter how good the teacher is, it is up to the student to put forth the necessary effort.

"Iron Will"—The "iron will" gives us spiritual power. The study of the martial art is a real commitment both mentally and physically. All technical skills are temporary; they *must* be practiced to be maintained.

Justification—The reason for training in the martial arts. The God-given right to protect oneself. You need not justify your actions. Just keep training hard! People who criticize you for your involvement in the martial arts are jealous and probably too lazy for any exercise. We call this disease T.R., or Terminal Relaxation. This is the Chinese Goju terminology for the good ole laziness religion. You need no reason to keep fit; just pride in yourself.

Knowledge—Knowledge is not yours until you give it to someone else. Teachers make the difference . . . the system is the solution. The knowledge is mental, the application of this knowledge physical. Modernization is the intelligent choice! Always use your bio-computer—knowledge is positive action.

Logic—Logic is necessary when making critical decisions. Always think before reacting to any positive or negative stimulus. Your powers of reason elevate you from just another animal to an aware individual. Remember, Speed + Timing + Focus = Maximum Effort.

Meditation—This is necessary to maintain the proper equilibrium between the bio-computer and the spiritual self. In the martial arts we use zen for meditation. The ability to coordinate the mind and body to work together is a form of zen meditation. Meditation gives you self-awareness.

Necessities—These are the priorities of our lives. Speed and flexibility are the necessary components of effective self-defense application. Use only what is necessary!

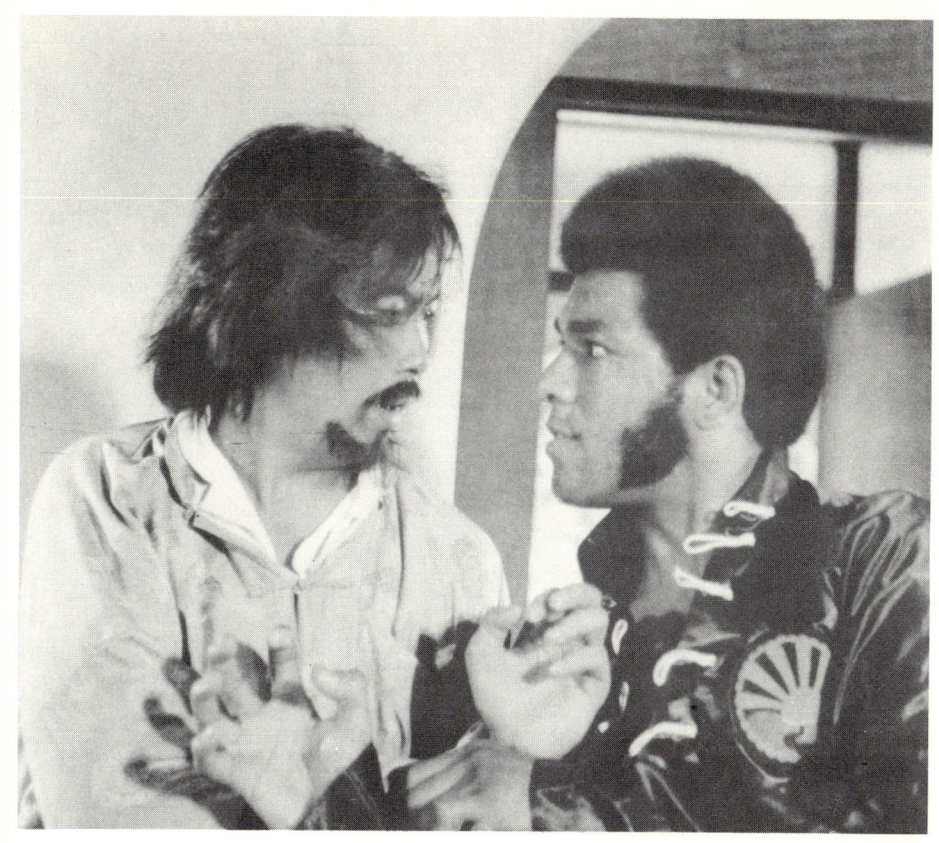

Objectivity—Objective analysis is the ability to think clearly, taking in all factors involved and making the right decision. Simply, understanding the situation and formulating the correct solution to the confrontation.

Patience—Patience is a virtue! Always relax and put forth your best effort. Everything takes time—time to understand and time to practice the skill. Remember, patience is also a form of concentration.

Quitters—Quitters never win, winners never quit! It is necessary to practice all skills to maintain physical and mental abilities. Without continual maintenance, our skills would disappear.

Reality—This is different for everyone. We all live our separate realities. But reality means unchanging truth. What is, is; what isn't, isn't. In the real world, health, wealth, and knowledge are reality. Maintain your balance in the sea of life. The smart fighter will never hesitate to change tactics to implement the correct technique at the correct time. Conserve your energy for the impact force, and always maintain a positive mental attitude throughout life.

Speed—Speed is the amount of time between a stimulus and the reaction to it. Mental attitude and physical conditioning are the key points. Speed amplifies hit power.

Timing—Timing is the ability to use your bio-computer to calculate the speed of the offensive technique and react with the proper block/counter mechanisms. Perfect techniques thrown at the wrong time have no meaning. Know your capabilities—your hands will always be faster than your legs! Speed is increased by the use of proper training methods.

Unity—Unity is the right combination of mental, physical, and spiritual energies to acquire inner tranquility.

Variables—These are limitless! Be creative, use anything that works. Remember, your opponent is capable of anything. Always stay in control of yourself and your environment. In training, practice good form in technique delivery. Legs work best to the lower areas, hands work best from the middle areas upward. Never become one-sided. Practice all techniques from both sides.

Weapons—Weapons are the various hand and leg techniques, but our best weapon is our mind's potential. Be aware! Always maintain life-support systems. Use your weapons only for self-defense under emergency situations.

X—X is the Unknown Factor in life. I have devised an equation to clarify this principle: A = Variables (How many are involved in the encounter? Are they armed or unarmed? Physical dimensions big or small?). B = Bio-computer (the iron will and practical self-defense mechanisms). Simply, creative imagination and systematic logic activate the correct self-defense devices. C = Conditioning. Are you physically and psychologically ready for any confrontation (the mental attitude of your attackers versus your martial skills)? X = The outcome of a life-and-death situation. Remember the first law of martial arts reality: Never get hit! To determine the outcome, hold fast to this equation:

$$\frac{A \times C}{B} = X \qquad X \text{ is the outcome.}$$

Yielding—Yield to force! Never resist force directly; force must be deflected or controlled. I believe in the principle of gong and yau. Gong is external force, yau internal force. Gong and yau coexist, complementing each other. It is like two halves of a circle which join to make a complete whole.

Zen—Zen is the ability to enjoy life in health and peace. Martial arts are my religion and zen is my way of life. Zen meditation has enabled me to maintain a positive mental attitude throughout my life. You can be in control of your destiny! I learned a great deal about zen from Grandmaster Peter Urban, Tenth Degree Red Belt. He taught me that zen is reality. The *Z* is for "zeal," the *E* is for "energy," the *N* for "nowness." Today is tomorrow: What you do today affects your tomorrow. Remember, the natural laws of cause and effect apply to everything.

Appendix
The World Masters in Action Awards

THE UNIVERSITY OF MARTIAL ARTS
"HALL OF FAME"
1965 TO 1981

1965
Best Fighter Frank Ruiz
Best Kata Toyotaro Miyazaki
Best Weapons Ronald Duncan
Best Demonstration Tadashi Nakamura
and Shigeru Oyama
Martial Arts Pioneer Award
Peter Urban, S. Henry Cho,
Don Nagel, Maynard Minor
Superstar Award Ed Parker
Martial Arts Author Award
Mas Oyama, *This Is Karate*

1966
Best Fighter Thomas LaPuppet
Best Kata William Louie
Best Weapons Moses Powell
Best Demonstration Alan Lee
Sensei of the Year
George Cofield
Superstar Award C. K. Kim
Martial Arts Author Award
Ed Parker, *Kempo Karate*

1967
Best Fighter Chuck Norris
Best Kata Ronald Taganashi
Best Weapons Al Decascos
Best Demonstration Hidy Ochai
Sensei of the Year
Richard Kim
Superstar Award Mike Stone
Martial Arts Author Award
Bruce Lee, *Chinese Gung Fu*

1968
Best Fighter Joe Lewis
Best Kata Chuck Merriman
Best Weapons Tadashi Yamashita
Best Demonstration Tiger Kim
Sensei of the Year
Richard Chun
Superstar Award Malachi Lee
Martial Arts Author Award
Peter Urban, *The Karate Dojo*

1969
Best Fighter Ron Van Clief
Best Kata Toyotaro Miyazaki
Best Weapons Wai Hong
Best Demonstration Bruce Lee
Sensei of the Year
Leo Fong
Superstar Award Joe Hayes
Martial Arts Author Award
Mas Oyama, *Advanced Karate*

1970
Best Fighter Chan Goon Tai
Best Kata William Oliver
Best Weapons (Gung fu)
Myung Sup Kim
Best Demonstration (Japanese Karate)
George Cofield
Sensei of the Year
Frank Ruiz
Sifu of the Year
David Chow
Best Weapons (Japanese Karate)
James Roberts
Best Demonstration (Gung fu)
Daniel Pai
Superstar Award Louis Delgado
Martial Arts Author Award
S. Henry Cho, *Korean Karate*

1971
Best Fighter Fred Miller
Best Kata Tayari Gasel
Best Weapons (Gung fu)
Gin foo Mark
Best Demonstration Owen Watson
Sensei of the Year
Gary Alexander
Sifu of the Year
Ming Pai
Best Weapons (Japanese Karate)
Hidy Ochai
Superstar Award Chuck Norris
Martial Arts Author Award
Richard Chun, *Moo Duk Kwan*

1972
Best Fighter Ron Marchini
Best Kata Eric Lee
Best Weapons Ron Van Clief
Best Demonstration Bruce Lee
Sensei of the Year
Steve Saunders
Sifu of the Year
Chan Chou
Superstar Award Fumio Demura
Martial Arts Author Award
Leo Fong, *Hung Gar*

1973
Best Fighter John Davis
Best Kata William Oliver
Best Weapons Tonny Kusotomo
Best Demonstration Ron Van Clief
Sensei of the Year
Pete Siringano
Sifu of the Year
Bucksam Kong
Superstar Award Benny Uriquidez
Martial Arts Author Award
Dan Inosanto, *Arnis and Escrima*

1974
Best Fighter Earl Monroe
Best Kata William Oliver
Best Weapons Eric Lee
Best Demonstration William Louie
Sensei of the Year
Nick Adler
Sifu of the Year
Curtis Wong
Superstar Award
Bill "Superfoot" Wallace
Martial Arts Author Award
Herman Petras, *Martial Arts Handbook*

1975
Best Fighter Errol Bennet
Best Kata Sheldon Wilkins
Best Weapons Jason Lau
Best Demonstration Karriem Allah
Sensei of the Year
Bob Cuccinello
Sifu of the Year
Ralph Mitchell
Superstar Award David Carradine
Martial Arts Author Award
Jay T. Will, *Kempo Self-Defense*

1978
Best Fighter Steve Fisher
Best Kata Chaka Zulu
Best Weapons Robert Crosson
Best Demonstration Jason Lau
Sensei of the Year
Emil Farkas
Sifu of the Year
Leung Ting
Superstar Award Sheldon Wilkins
Martial Arts Author Award
Maurice J. Miller, Photo-journalist

1976
Best Fighter Dominic Valera
Best Kata Alex Sternberg
Best Weapons Jason Pai Piao
Best Demonstration Charles Bonet
Sensei of the Year
Ed Parker
Sifu of the Year
George Crayton
Superstar Award Malia Decascos
Martial Arts Author Award
George Mattson, *Okinawan Karate*

1979
Best Fighter
Benny "The Jet" Uriquidez
Best Kata George Chung
Best Weapons George Crayton
Best Demonstration Robert Crosson
Sensei of the Year
Louis Neglia
Sifu of the Year
Leung Ting
Superstar Award Gerald Robbins
Martial Arts Photographer Award
Joe Griffith

1977
Best Fighter Bill Wallace
Best Kata Milagros Tirado
Best Weapons Dick Chan
Best Demonstration Duncan Leung
Sensei of the Year
Chuck Norris
Sifu of the Year
Tayari Casel
Superstar Award Cynthia Rothrock
Martial Arts Author Award
John McGee, Photo-journalist

1980
Best Fighter Keith Vitali
Best Kata William Oliver
Best Weapons Tommy May
Best Demonstration Rico Mercado
Sensei of the Year
Nick Adler
Sifu of the Year
William Chung
Superstar Award Chuck Norris
Martial Arts Author Award
Emil Farkas, *The Martial Arts Catalog*

1981

Best Fighter
Amateur William Oliver, Bill Wallace
Professional David Claudio
Best Kata Toyotaro Miyazaki
Best Weapons Anthony Chan
Best Demonstration Ronald Duncan
Sensei of the Year
Peter Urban
Sifu of the Year
Anthony Lau
Superstar Award Chuck Norris
Martial Arts Author Award
Al Weiss, *Clan of Death: The Ninja;*
Joe Hyams, *Zen in the Martial Arts*

Honorable Mention for Contribution to the World of Martial Arts, 1981:

Aaron Banks, Steve Valencia, Don Wilson, Herbie Thompson, Ron Austin, Bill Wallace, Ray McCallum, Cookie Melendez, Graciela Casillas, Sidney Filson, Mike Warren, Paul Vizzio, Mike Bell, Demetrius Havanas, Cynthia Rothrock, Maurice Miller, and Miligros Tirado.

INDEX

Advanced self-defense, 161–69
Aiki-choke, 119, 121, 129, 136, 150, 166
Aiki jitsu, 9, 85, 119, 132, 143, 147, 166
    see also Aiki-choke; Aiki-lever
Aiki-lever, 146, 165, 166
Alphabet of martial arts, 171–80
Animal forms in self-defense, 161–69
    see also specific animal forms, e.g. Snake style;
       Tiger style
Arm lever, 109
Arnis, 162
Attacking, 58
    see also Combat; Counterattacking; Self-defense
Attack zones, 104, 106

Bear style, 161
Belt-ranking system, 16
Bermudez, Marion, 114
Black Belts, 16, 117
Black Dragon Blocking System, 55–68
    applications, 58–68, 125, 127, 130, 144
    form and technique, 56–58
    low palm-up block with upper
       sunfist strike, 62–63
    palm-up block against upper body punching, 65–66
    palm-up block and grab with sunfist attack, 67–68
    palm-up block with iron palm strike, 60–61
    rising block with sunfist, 59–60, 127, 131
    side palm block with middle sunfist punch, 64–65
Black Dragon Gung Fu system, 51, 74
    see also Black Dragon Blocking System
Black Tiger of Shantung, 46
Black Tiger style, 46, 47
Block-and-counter application, 15, 104, 107
    see also Black Dragon Blocking System;
       Self-defense
Blocking, 13, 14, 58, 91, 143
    see also Black Dragon Blocking System;
       Self-defense
Breathing, 18, 58
    see also individual exercises and techniques
Brown Belts, 16, 117

Cardiovascular exercises, 18, 23, 143
"Chamber" position, 14–15, 38, 72, 73, 76, 77, 83, 84,
    92, 93, 120, 145
Chan, President, 79
Chan Chou, 79
Chan Goon Tai, 79, 105
Chen Sing, 105
Chiang Cheh, 79
Children, martial arts education for, 153–159
    defense against attempted front grab, 156–57
    defense against strangers, 158–59
    defense against wrist grab, 154–56
China, 10, 11, 41
    see also Chinese Goju

Chinese Arts Association of Hong Kong, 79
Chinese Goju, 11–12, 15, 28, 37, 53, 91, 102, 104
    alphabet of martial arts, 171–80
    belt-ranking system, 16
    hand techniques in, 25, 28
    leg techniques in, 72, 79, 80, 83, 92, 94
    self-defense and, 115–69 passim
    see also specific techniques
Chinese wrestling, 150
Chi sao, 82
Choke(s), 147
    aiki-, 119, 121, 129, 136, 150, 166
    front, countering the, 120–21
Chaun fa, See Kung fu
Chung Wah Martial Arts Association, 79
Coiling snake technique, 82, 149, 165
    see also Aiki-Choke
Combat, 15, 113, 114
    children and, 153, 158
    tactics and strategy, 106–11
Constant forward motion, 53, 61, 66, 78, 91, 108, 109,
    116, 119, 122, 124, 126, 134, 146, 148, 150, 164,
    168, 173
Constant motion principle, 75, 138, 139
Constant technique flow, 67, 119, 123, 125, 139
Coordination, 17, 23, 53
Counterattacking, 13–14, 91
    see also Black Dragon Blocking System;
       Self-defense
Crane style, 41, 161
Critical distance, 13–14, 15, 25, 43

Daruma, 10
Delgado, Lewis, 86
Discipline, 17, 22
Doctor, consulting your, 18
Dojang, 18
Dojo, 18, 104
Double-hand striking, 44
    double tiger claw, 51–52, 85, 111, 123, 125, 128, 129,
       137, 139, 145, 150, 155, 164, 165
    double wrist attack, 120
Dragon palm 133, 134
Dragon style, 161
Dragon tail sweep and iron broom
    combination, 167–69
Duncan, Ronald, 150

Eagle Claw style, 79, 161
Elbow strike, 33–34, 95, 109, 110, 111, 119, 135, 137, 138
Elephant style, 161
Emotional content, 17
Endurance, 18, 20, 27
"Escape and evasion" training, 85, 156
Exercising, 17–18, 143
    jackknife, 21
    jumping rope, 23

points to remember, 22
push-up, 20
Eye training, 14

Face front punch, countering the, 91
Flexibility, 17, 57, 104
Focus, 13, 14
Fong, Leo, 162
Forms or sets, 46
Front choke, self-defense against, 120–21
Front grab, self-defense against, 146-47, 156-57
Front heel kick, 72–75, 78, 157
Front kick, 83–85, 116, 120, 155
Front punch, straight, self-defense against, 115–17
Funakoshi, Gichin, 11

Garcia, Darnell, 162
Goju. See Chinese Goju
Golden Harvest Film studios, 105
Goti, 150
Grabbing technique, 77, 78, 89, 91, 93, 107, 135, 138
Green Belts, 16, 117
Gung fu. see Kung fu

Hammer strike, overhead, self-defense against, 144–45
Hand techniques, 14, 25–53, 71, 104, 131
  double tiger claw, 51–52, 85, 111, 123, 125, 128, 129, 137, 139, 145, 150, 155, 164, 165
  elbow strike, 33–34, 95, 109, 110, 111, 119, 135, 137, 138
  hook punch, 35–36
  iron palm, 14, 37–38, 60–61, 121, 125, 126, 140, 149
  monkey elbow, 39–40, 119, 122, 138, 139
  multiple leg and, in combination, 108–11
  snake fist, 14, 41–45
  sunfist, 14, 26–31, 57, 58, 59–60, 62–68, 78, 106, 125, 127, 131
  tiger claw, 14, 46–50, 93, 121, 125, 126, 138, 147, 157, 163, 164
  twin sunfist, 31–32
Holds, 143, 147
Hong Kong, 79, 105
Hooking blocks, 116
Hook kick, 95–98
Hook punch, 35–36
Horse style, 161
Hung Gar style, 79

Instant strike force, 66, 68
Instep kick. See Low round kick
Instructors, 16, 18, 103, 105
Introduction to martial arts, 9–16
Ippons, 115–69 passim
  ippon kumite, 104
Iron broom and dragon tail sweeps combination, 167–69
Iron elbow, 14
Iron palm, 14, 37–38, 121, 125, 126, 140, 149
  palm-up block with, 60–61
Iron will training, 27, 150, 175
Isokinetics, 18
Isometrics, 18
Isotonics, 18

Jackknife, 21
Japan, 11, 85
Japanese Goju, 86
Judo, 17
Jumping rope, 23

Kanogogi, Rusty, 113
Karate, 9, 17, 25, 46, 53, 91, 113, 143, 147, 150
  leg techniques, 86
  origins of, 9–10, 11
  purposes of, 12–13
  see also specific techniques
"Kata," 13, 46, 86, 159
"Kempo," 11, 86
Kicking. See Leg techniques
Kim, Dr. Richard, 11
Knee to groin, 135, 136, 149
Knife attacks, self-defense against, 124–29
Korean forms of martial arts, 71, 113
Kung fu (Gung fu), 9, 10, 11, 17, 18, 25, 41, 46, 71, 79, 82, 92, 147, 161, 162
  films, 79, 102, 105, 162
  origins of, 10
  see also specific techniques
Kwoon, 18
Kyoshi, 16

Law of survival, Van Clief's, 107
Laws of martial arts sciences, Van Clief's, 102
Lee, Bruce, 41, 71, 79, 82, 104, 161, 162
Leg techniques, 14–15, 71–98, 104, 131
  front heel kick, 72–75, 78, 157
  front kick, 83–85, 116, 120, 155
  hook kick, 95–98
  low round kick, 75–78, 91, 108, 167
  monkey knee, 79–82, 123, 128, 129, 139, 149, 155, 164
  multiple, in combination, 106–11
  round kick, 93–95, 106, 108, 117, 125, 126
  side kick, 86–93, 107, 109, 117, 118, 128, 131, 133, 145, 156, 157, 159
Leopard style, 161
Leung Ting, Sifu, 41, 79, 162
Levers, 107, 110, 143, 146, 147, 165, 166
  see also Arm lever; Wrist lever
Lewis, Joe, 86
Liu, John, 105
Locks, 143, 147
Low round kick, 75–78, 91, 108, 167

Mao Ying, Angela, 114
Maximum Effort, 60, 66
Melendez, Cookie, 114
Mental attitude, positive, 61, 66
Middle-section front kick, monkey-elbow applied against, 40
Miyagi, Chojun, 11
Miyazaki, Toyotaro, 86
Monkey elbow, 39–40, 119, 122, 138, 139
Monkey knee, 79–82, 123, 128, 129, 139, 149, 155, 164
Monkey style, 79, 161, 164, 166
Monkey sweep, 167–69
Moo Duk Kwan, 71
Muscle strength and tone, 23

Ninja, 85, 86, 119, 136, 150
Nisei Goju System, 11

Okinawa, 9–10, 11, 113
Okinawa Goju, 86
Opening, creating an, 15
Origins of martial arts, 9–12
Overhead strikes with weapons, self-defense against, 127-29, 144–45
Oyama, Mas, 11
Ozawa, Sumiko, 113–14

Pak Mei (White Eyebrow) style, 79
Palm-up block, 58
   and grab with sunfist attack, 67–68
   with iron palm strike, 60–61
   with middle sunfist punch, 64–65
   against upper body punching, 65–66
   with upper sunfist strike, low, 62–63
Peterson, Lorna, 114
Phoenix attacks, 132–40
   countering the wrist grab, 136–40
Phoenix style, 161
Piao, Jason Pai, 41, 79
Pentjak, 11
Physical fitness, 17–18, 19, 114
Power, 13, 17, 26, 27
Praying Mantis style, 161
Presas, Remy, 162
Progressive resistance, 27
Psycho-physical conditioning process. See Warm up
Purple Belts, 16, 117
Push-up, 20

Rattans, 162
Rear grab, self-defense against, 118–19, 148–50
Red Belts, 16
Renshi, 16
Reverse heel kick. See Hook kick
Ripping techniques, 49
Rising block, 59–60, 127, 131, 144
Rocket punch. See Sunfist
Rosenstein, Harry, 11
Rotary punching. See Sunfist
Rothrock, Cynthia, 114
Round kick, 93–95, 106, 108, 117, 125, 126
   see also Low round kick
Ruiz, Frank, 11

Schools, 17, 105
Self-defense, 102, 104
   advanced, using animal forms, 161-69
   for children, 154–59
   for senior citizens, 143–50
   for women, 113–40
Senior citizens, self-defense for, 143–50
   against front grab, 146–47
   against overhead hammer strike, 144–45
   against rear grab, 148–50
Sensei, 16, 105
Set-up, 123
Shaolin Monastery, 46
Shauble, Leona, 114

Shaw Brothers studio, 79, 105
Shin kick. See Low round kick
Shock shove. See Iron palm
Shorinryu, 86
Shotokan, 86
Side grab, self-defense against, 122–23
Side kick, 86–93, 107, 109, 117, 118, 128, 131, 133, 145, 156, 157, 159
   countering the, 90–91
   in motion, 92–93
   practical application of, 89
   target variables, 90
Silat, 11
Slap block. See Palm-up block
Snake fist, 14, 41–45
   attack and control, 43–44
   attacks in motion, 45
   practical application of, 43
Snake style, 41–45, 82, 133, 147, 148, 161, 164, 165
Snap kicks, 85, 86
Southeast Asia, 10–11, 41
Sparring. See Combat
Speed, 13, 14, 17, 26, 53, 55, 104, 178
Stamina, 17, 20, 23, 27
"Sticky hands," 162
Strangers, children and, 158–59
Strategy and tactics, 102–11
   attack zones, 104, 106
   multiple arm and leg techniques in combination, 108–111
   multiple leg techniques in combination, 106–107
Strength. See Power
Sunfist, 14, 26–31, 57, 58, 78, 106, 125
   low palm-up block with upper, 62–63
   palm up block against upper body, 65–66
   palm up block and grab with, attack, 67–68
   practical application, 31
   rising block with, 59–60, 127, 131
   side palm block with middle, 64–65
   supplementary progressive resistance, 27–28
   twin, 32–33
Sweeps, 147, 167–69

Tactics. See Strategy and tactics
Tae Kwon Do, 9, 17, 18, 71, 86, 113
Taganashi, Reverend Ronald, 86
Tang Soo Do, 71
Technical applications chart, Van Clief method of, 103
"Thai boxers," 82, 138
Thrust kicks, 85, 86, 89
Tiger claw, 14, 46–50, 93, 121, 125, 126, 138, 147, 157, 163, 164
   double, 51–52, 85, 111, 123, 125, 128, 129, 137, 139, 145, 150, 155, 164, 165
   practical applications, 48–50
Tiger-Claw School, 46
Tiger palm strike, 139
Tiger style, 46–53, 161, 162, 164, 165
   movements of the tiger, 51–53
Tiger tail. See Side kick
Timing, 13, 178
Tirado, Milagros, 114
Training aids, 161, 162
Trapping hands, 82
Twin sunfist, 31–32

United States, 11–12
Urban, Peter, 11, 22, 104, 180
U.S.A. Goju, 11

Van Clief, Ron, 12
    law of survival, 107
    laws of martial arts sciences, 102
    method of technical applications chart, 103

Wai Hong, Sifu, 46
Wang Yu, Jimmy 105
Warm up, 17–23
    jackknife, 21
    jumping rope, 23
    points to remember, 22
    purposes of, 17, 23
    push up, 20
Weapon attacks, self-defense against, 124–29, 144–45
Weight loss, 23
Weight training, 27
White Belts, 16, 117
White Crane style, 79
White Eyebrow style, 79
White snake, 42, 134, 164
Wing Tsun style of gung fu, 41, 71, 79, 82, 162

Women, self-defense for, 113–40
    countering the wrist grab, 136–40
    famous martial artists, 114
    against the front choke, 120–21
    against the front lunge knife attack, 124–26
    against the overhead knife attack, 127–29
    Phoenix attacks, 132–40
    against the rear grab, 118–19
    against the side grab, 122–23
    against the straight front punch, 115–17
Wooden man, 161, 162
World Masters in Action Awards, 181–84
Wrist grab, 53, 85, 134
    countering, Phoenix attacks, 136–40
    self-defense for children
        against, 154–56
Wrist lever, 107

X, 179

Yamaguchi, Gogen, 11
Yielding, 180

Zen, 12, 86, 176, 180